RAGING
Gracefully

Smart Women on Life, Love, and Coming into Your Own

Edited by
Jennifer "Gin" Sander
Author of *The Martini Diet*

Adams Media
Avon, Massachusetts

Published by
Adams Media, an F+W Publications Company
57 Littlefield Street, Avon, MA 02322
www.adamsmedia.com

ISBN 10: 1-59337-621-9
ISBN 13: 978-1-59337-621-5

Printed in the United States of America.

J I H G F E D C B A

Library of Congress Cataloging-in-Publication Data
Raging gracefully / edited by Jennifer "Gin" Sander.
p. cm.
ISBN 1-59337-621-9
1. Women--United States--Anecdotes. 2. Middle-aged women--United States--Anecdotes. I. Sander, Jennifer Basye
HQ1421.R34 2006
305.244'20973--dc22
2006014719

This publication is designed to provide accurate and authoritative informa-tion with regard to the subject matter covered. It is sold with the understand-ing that the publisher is not engaged in rendering legal, accounting, or other professional advice. If legal advice or other expert assistance is required, the services of a competent professional person should be sought.
   —From a *Declaration of Principles* jointly adopted by a Committee of the American Bar Association and a Committee of Publishers and Associations

Many of the designations used by manufacturers and sellers to distinguish their product are claimed as trademarks. Where those designations appear in this book and Adams Media was aware of a trademark claim, the desig-nations have been printed with initial capital letters.

Brush image © Ken Reid/Getty Images
Woman image © Meiklejohn/UK Gianenelli/Images.com

This book is available at quantity discounts for bulk purchases.
For information, please call 1-800-872-5627.

ACKNOWLEDGMENTS

I'd like to thank all of the incredible women who submitted stories to this collection. It was an enjoyable task to read the words of such talented writers.

And I'd especially like to thank Sue Pearson Atkinson for her help as story editor. Her contacts, suggestions, and input were there whenever I needed them.

CONTENTS

INTRODUCTION

I tried to thread a needle this morning. Couldn't do it. Ended up using that iron-on patch stuff instead to fix the small hole in my black sweater—thankfully, the iron was big enough for me to spot in the cupboard. I also managed to find the phone and call for an appointment with the eye doctor.

I'm getting older, and I'm guessing you are too. Heavy sigh. All my life I've loudly claimed not to be afraid of growing old. There have been incredible older women in my life whom I've long planned to emulate in my later years—Nina, whose favorite colors were purple and pink and who therefore used pink plastic shower curtains as drapes in her rambling purple cliff-side Victorian. Willoughby, who loudly announced that the only public room in her house was the living room and she simply couldn't be bothered to keep anything more than that clean on a daily basis. Tall and thin, she dressed in safari clothes and drove a Willy's Jeep with great style and panache. Fay, the wrinkled next-door neighbor who drew me aside in high school and whispered that I should always have all of my diamonds X-rayed to minimize the chance a disreputable jeweler might switch them on me. Important information every sixteen-year-old should have. Wonderful women, aging with style, living life on their own terms and loudly proclaiming that public opinion be damned.

What I realize now as the years slip by is that I only knew these women when they were *already old*. Nina, Willoughby, and Fay had already passed through that awkward phase of actually *getting older,* of watching the wrinkles arrive and hearing the compliments grow silent. Of wondering if they were still attractive to someone, anyone . . . Chances are they were as troubled by aging as I am and as you are too. But they had already made peace with their faces and their bodies and their eyes. You and I are still squinting our way towards our futures as bold older women.

At this point I'd describe myself as an aging pretty girl, the fading high school beauty with a bathroom full of the latest potions and creams, each promising faster and more obvious results. I'm so looking forward to being a powerful older woman, a strong woman who has put all of this behind her, but I seem to have sunk into the self-obsessed trenches, peering with worry and concern at the arrival of each and every new wrinkle. Getting older isn't just about our changing looks. In an effort to focus on other parts of growing older, I began to look for other role models, other women's stories to help keep me focused on matters of greater importance than whether my faded high-school uniform will still fit come my thirtieth reunion this summer.

As I've wandered out into the world asking other women how their lives have changed over the years, it seems I've heard about everything *but* looks. About how this is the time to shed all those possessions that hold us back and literally sail into a new way of living. About making the decision to become someone else. About learning a new skill, taking a new test, or—okay—maybe trying a new hair color! Raging gracefully. Not "aging" gracefully? Well really, who does want to age, after all? Instead, let us all roar with pleasure, rage at the fates, or sing out in honor of the world around us.

This book isn't about anger at growing older; it's about learning that the things that stay with us are the things that challenge us the most in life. The stories here celebrate that this is a time when our confidence grows. When we truly emerge with a solid sense of self. As young girls, we all floundered and flopped around in life, trying things out and sometimes falling flat on our youthful faces. As women, we can sometimes reach back into our past for a new way to operate now.

Just recently, I realized that I could "woo" my young son Julian in the exact same way I seduced countless boyfriends, by adopting their interests as my own. You got this advice from your mom, too—*If you want a boy to like you, take an interest in his interests, ask him about himself.* So in my teens, I put aside what I liked and took an interest in baseball, tennis, punk rock, and, best of all, auto racing. In my twenties and thirties I expected men to take up my interests, and they did quite willingly. Okay, no one ever took up opera, but most of my boyfriends seemed happy to hunt for used books and drink strong coffee in outdoor cafes. My husband has his hobbies (steam trains, Ultimate Frisbee), and I have mine (needlepoint, and oh yes, opera).

But keeping the interest of a ten-year-old boy is quite a different story. So I have taken up surfing. I can also speak knowledgably on major skateboarding brands, and I know a thing or two about Green Day (all that time in punk clubs has come in handy after all). Once it seemed insecure to adapt to someone else's needs, but I now have the confidence to do it again.

When gathering the stories to share here in *Raging Gracefully,* my coeditor Sue Pearson Atkinson and I asked women about three things—life, love, and coming into their own. Was there a time when you realized that you needed to make a big change *and* had the courage to do it? At our age, there is wisdom that comes with experience, and everyone had something to say. Although we hope to help you grow older with a smile on your face, not all of the stories we've collected here are funny. Some of them contain life lessons learned quite painfully. Even the amusing stories remind us that what stays with us and enriches us are the very things that challenge us the most.

Read on, and discover the treats that await you! And do come and visit me at my blog—The Black Dress Manifesto (*www.blackdressmanifesto.blogspot.com*). That is where I, an ordinary woman, am trying very, very hard to find glamour, wisdom, and a good wrinkle cream with which to face the coming years. Red hats and purple dresses? Oh, please, ladies! We can rage more gracefully than that! I'm counting on a well-cut black dress and a very dry martini to see me through the next few decades. Hope you can join me!

Jennifer "Gin" Sander

FUZZY-SWEATER
Feminists

Over and over I've heard women say these same words whenever the conversation touched on topics like girls playing sports, who would fill the next Supreme Court vacancy, or what happens when a woman earns more than her man. Every time, at least one woman says "Well, I'm not a feminist, but . . ."

I smile and say, "Me? I am a feminist. Oh yes!"

Here's how this feminist spent her day—taking a sick child to the doctor, vacuuming the living room, running a load of whites through the washer and dryer, and baking a loaf of whole wheat bread. (Lest you hate me right off the bat, I will admit to using a bread machine.) While waiting out the spin cycle I read the obituary of the writer Elizabeth Janeway. The headline in my local paper identified her as "Elizabeth Janeway, feminist author, " and went on to say that "among feminists, Mrs. Janeway was a less strident but still powerful voice." *Less strident?* Where did this notion come from that feminists are strident?

It certainly seems prevalent nowadays on the radio and television airwaves, from one end of the dial to the other. Would the description of my typical day come as a surprise to Rush Limbaugh or any other of the media men who trumpets loudly about "femi-Nazis?" How do they imagine that a feminist spends her time? In their view, I should perhaps have been at the Bush inauguration holding a sign of some sort, or busily composing a letter to Harvard's president protesting his recent remarks about why there aren't more women scientists. Instead, I had a house to clean.

How is it that the word "feminist" came to be so unappealing? I have a theory, formed in the long-ago days when I was a political consultant. In any kind of a debate or face-off between two ideas or candidates, the person who manages to define the terms under discussion gains the upper hand and generally wins. Most recently, we saw this play out in the 2004 presidential election. John Kerry's thoughtfulness and measured consideration of the issues was defined as wishy-washy, and George Bush's much different approach was portrayed as strong and firm. Personally, I'd like George Bush to be a little less strident. Perhaps he can take a page from the life of Mrs. Janeway.

Over the years, folks like Rush have reshaped the meaning of the word "feminist" to the general public, and as a result, many women (and most young girls) are reluctant to define themselves that way. A bunch of loud-mouthed man-haters, who'd want to be associated with *them*?

Man-haters? Odd, but in all of the years I spent at a girls' high school in the seventies, a women's college in the eighties, and in the world of business in the nineties, never once did I hear anyone denounce men. Maybe I was out of the room at the time, talking to a boyfriend.

To me, the idea of being a feminist has never included the notion that men were an enemy of any kind. Rather than allowing the word to be tarnished by negative stereotypes, I thought, why not focus instead on what it really means?

Curious, I turned to the bookshelf. I first sought the advice of the thick and reassuringly heavy Random House dictionary, an edition published in 1966. Most of us would associate the year 1966 with the early stirrings of the modern feminist movement in America. And this dictionary defined "feminism" in a very mild way: *the doctrine advocating social and political rights of women equal to those of men.*

Mine is a two-writer household, with many a dictionary on hand. Rummaging through the shelves a second time I found a newer one, the 1998 Merriam-Webster Collegiate edition. Thirty-two years later, feminism was now defined this way: *the theory of the political, economic, and social equality of the sexes.* Glad to see that money has been added to the parity equation. That was a primary motivator for Elizabeth Janeway too, according to her obit. The wife of economist Eliot Janeway, she was no doubt well aware of the importance of money and her obituary pointed out that "she wanted equal pay for equal work."

Both of the definitions sound perfectly positive to me. Each gives an evenhanded description of a possible relationship between the sexes, not a damnation of the circumstances that made it necessary decades ago to strive for equality in the first place. I'm forty-seven myself, and my own life parallels many of the advances won by the women's movement in the seventies. I just bobbed along and ended up on shore exactly when the wave of progress broke. Unwilling to focus only on my own version of feminism, I polled a few friends—a woman in her sixties, a woman in her fifties, and a woman in her early forties. I guessed that each woman's age and experiences would shape her willingness to describe herself as a feminist. Here's what I heard when I asked these three women if they were feminists:

Judith: "Of course! I believe that women have rights equal to men."

Barbara: "Of course! I'm proud of it. The suffragettes were amazing and we have so much to be grateful for. By calling myself a feminist I feel connected to their work. Lucky us."

Donna: "No! Well, some parts I agree with . . . like that women deserve the same rights as men, but I just don't think that they deserve to play in the NFL."

Huh. I missed the part about playing in the NFL as one of the things feminists wanted. Guess I was outside of the room again that time while all this high-level political planning was going on behind my back, talking in the hallway to yet another cute guy. Chances are he was a football player, too.

Can you guess who is who by their answers? Judith is in her sixties, Barbara is in her fifties, and yes, Donna is forty-one. I tremble to think what the response might have been if I'd polled a few women in their twenties.

In my writing career I've climbed on many a soapbox to urge women to take charge of their money and their careers. Build up your net worth! Build a business of your own! How many ways can you write about money, though? As a topic it had worn thin. In the past two years I've morphed from writing books and articles about women and money to writing about small luxuries, moderate indulgence, and losing weight. Instead of addressing large groups of women on the topics of investing and savvy marketing, I now stand on the stage in a bright pink St. John suit and giggle about martinis and massages.

About midway through my talk on small and inexpensive ways that women can take care of themselves, I begin to refer to myself as a "fuzzy-sweater feminist." The fuzzy-sweater part is a reference to my book *Wear More Cashmere: 151 Luxurious Ways to Pamper Your Inner Princess.* Not exactly what you would mistake for a feminist creed. Ah, but you would be wrong. Buried amidst the suggestions on how to feel like a movie star (wear high-heeled mules and wrap a sarong around your hips, instant glam!) and an inexpensive way to duplicate the very expensive hot-rock spa massage (a couple of rocks, a slow cooker, and some massage oil are all you need) are long passages in which I remind women that they have the ability to create the life they want rather than sit back and wait for someone else to do it for them. Empower that inner princess, honey.

The fuzzy-sweater feminist line always gets a laugh. Not only is my intention to get a laugh and a smile from the women and men in the room, but also (in as nonstrident a way as possible) to gently reclaim and rebrand the word feminist as, well, more feminine. Ultra feminine, in fact.

I extended the fuzzy-sweater feminist philosophy to losing weight in a recent diet book. A feminist diet book? Indulge me for a moment while I quote from the final chapter of *The Martini Diet: The Self-indulgent Way to a Thinner, More Fabulous You* (feel free to picture me standing before you in a bright pink suit, which you need to know that as a thrifty woman I bought secondhand):

> "As you may have begun to suspect, I'm a bit of a fuzzy-sweater feminist. Having started out as a junior lobbyist for a women's organization (even then I stalked the halls of the U.S. Capitol in perilously high heels, draped in silk, though with only the most demure single strand of pearls, and not the over-the-top twelve-foot strand I sport now) before wandering over to the business of books, I still harbor many of those same beliefs.

I still firmly believe that you and I are in charge of our own destinies, responsible for our own lives, and perfectly capable of creating our own opportunities. At the same time, I am appalled at the way women are actively discouraged from feeling pleased with the size and shape of their bodies. You must be strong in the face of the unhealthy media messages we receive minute by minute. You must be strong and courageous in the face of advertising that is designed to make you feel weak, inadequate, and imperfect without the advertiser's product."

The whole martini theme has to do with using restraint when approaching food, the same way that you only have one drink instead of six or seven. As you might suspect from the above excerpt, quite a bit of this diet-and-weight-loss book has to do with encouraging women to be proud of who they are now and not to absorb the constant negative messages we as women receive. Far more important than gaining entry to the NFL, I think. Like Judith and Barbara, I say "of course" I am a feminist. Should the dictionary folks get wind of my less-strident but still-powerful voice and ask me to help write the next entry, here is what I suggest:

Feminist: a woman who believes in her own unlimited strength and courage.

Ah! The buzzer on the dryer has sounded, and it smells like the bread might be done. Time for this fuzzy-sweater feminist to get back to her family. Here's hoping that my fuzzy sweater fits you, too.

JENNIFER "GIN" SANDER

Jennifer "Gin" Sander is the author of *Wear More Cashmere* and *The Martini Diet.* She lives with her husband Peter and sons Julian and Jonathan in Granite Bay, California.

HORSING
around

Whoever said, "You can't teach an old dog new tricks" didn't know any mothers in their forties.

Some women might think that by the time they enter their fifth decade, life should consist of settling into a plush chair, sipping tea, fiddling with charms on their bracelets, and niggling about the dust bunnies on the hardwood. But women in their forties who are engaged in the business of raising young children, discovering and channeling their interests, know there is not a moment for such peace. My life, for instance, will probably never include lounging on fancy chairs with idle time (or money) on my hands. And I have an old pony and a single one-hour trail ride to thank for it.

That hour changed my life immediately. When it was over, my eight-year-old daughter had turned from a dainty, lacy, tip-toeing, doll-carrying, quiet little girl into a horse. Boom. It was just like that. Like the split second it takes a lobster shell to turn bright red when dropped in a pot of boiling water. Or the flash of time where the kernel pops into popcorn.

It was sudden.

It started innocently enough. We were on our summer vacation, and I decided to splurge and send her on a first-ever horseback ride—a harmless hour, I thought. You may be asking yourself, "Could this be a bad idea?" The following true story will give you the chance to decide that for yourself.

Once my child got off that pony, she began to neigh, whinny, rear, buck, paw the ground, sniff, and make that loud nose-blowing sound. This would have been fine for an hour or so. A week, tops. But it continued into the school year, the next summer, even the next school year. And in no time two years had passed this way, and she was darn near ten years old.

Ever since that fateful ride, my daughter had been horse, rider, trainer, farrier—anything, as long as it's equine. She loped when other children would run. She insisted we follow all horse trailers we see on the highway. She cantered around the dining room table, the yard, up and down the driveway. Sitting two-point on the kitchen stool, she spoonlessly munched her bowls of oats. She ate carrots straight out of the refrigerator. She set up living-room jumps made of soup cans and broomsticks. Sometimes she even attached a rope like a longe line to her bicycle handlebars and ran it in circles around the driveway.

Then the pictures started appearing on her wall: horse hooves with those disgusting frogs, anatomy shots of the inner ear, the nasal passage of a horse, detailed drawings of horse intestines, listings of horse vocabulary words like pastern and hemlock. (Hemlock isn't really a horsy word, but you get the idea.)

This wouldn't have been so bad if she had been able to hold a meaningful conversation once in a while. But other than "Seabiscuit," the only words I heard from this once-intelligible being were words that had no meaning to anybody who wasn't, like my daughter, a horse. And to think that all I had ever wanted out of life was a sweet little pink ballerina child . . .

I finally concluded I had given birth to a horse trapped inside a girl's body.

The folks at the stable tell me this is normal. It happens every once in a while. You've heard of the phenomenon yourself: They're called "horse people." That's what we are now. I hear the other moms saying it in hushed whispers, "Oh, they're horse people." Like we're extraterrestrials, visiting their Planet Soccer.

Bucking that soccer trend (or being absolutely nuts), I realized that this good mother must foster her child's interests. So come my daughter's tenth birthday, I bit the bit and ponied up the pony.

I had no idea what I was doing. As a consequence, I arranged to have the new horse delivered to our suburban house. I suppose I had a fantasy about some wonderful, simple life with a horse as a pet. Luckily, I was with it just enough to find a pasture about a half-mile away where we could keep her. Still, I envisioned us walking said equine on a little leash home from her pasture every day after school, riding our bikes alongside her as she trotted down the street, sleeping curled up with her on the front lawn in the lazy afternoon sunshine, tying her to the mulberry tree while we washed the car, feeding her carrots through the kitchen window while I vacuumed. I convinced my husband I would be able to keep the house a whole lot cleaner just knowing we had a horse outside. This type of logic works on him.

I even planned to get a white gauzy dress, take the horse to the coast, and gallop her along the edge of the surf. Foam, mist, and salty air included. This, I told my husband, will make me feel a lot sexier. Over the edge with passion for me, he ripped open the want ads himself, looking for a horse—any horse. A very responsive guy, I say.

The horse we found was named Claire. With Claire in the family, going from a city girl to a horsewoman proved not to be too difficult. I traded in my car for a huge truck that travels two miles on each gallon of gas. I bought a horse trailer for a mere $15,000. I got a bunch of rubber boots, a couple of hay hooks, some tight pants, and a few velvet hats.

A few days after we got Claire, while my daughter was in school, I decided it was time to sneak in a little ride myself. My plan: lead Claire to the house from her pasture and then ride to a park about two miles away, where wonderful horse trails are said to wind along the American

River. I anticipated a relaxing three-hour ride. Looking back, I see now that this plan would have gone much better if I had ever ridden a horse before.

The first problem was putting Claire's bridle on. Though I had read up on this the night before and even brought along some diagrams, I have to admit that it took me two hours just to get the damn bit in her mouth. I finally managed it only after tying Claire to the truck's rearview mirror and climbing up on top of the truck cab so I could reach her snout, or whatever it's called. Needless to say, my pants got really dirty up there, and I started sweating pretty badly.

I really thought I knew how to get on a horse. I've watched plenty of movies, and I certainly remember riding the ponies at Fairy Tale Town when I was about three. I mean, how hard could it be? Put one foot in the stirrup and swing the other leg up and over the top, and wham, bango, zingo, you're off. Only it turned out that Claire was really tall. So tall I had to lift my foot up to my ear, which knocked my cell phone to the ground and induced a nasty cramp in the other leg, while trying to fit the foot into a stirrup that must have been made wrong in the first place. (I definitely planned to call that stirrup-manufacturing outfit first thing in the morning!) I was stuck like this for some time.

After I saw the neighbor peeking at me from behind her curtains, I decided to act like I had planned this whole thing. Gently, I arched my back toward the ground and gracefully tried flapping my arms. I came to a rest with my head on the grass, which was the perfect solution because then I could get both legs up, straighten out my angles, and free myself from that faulty stirrup.

Once again, I found an opportunity to be glad I had bought that expensive and gigantic truck. With Claire tied to the mirror, I again climbed up on the cab and dropped myself tenderly onto her back. I spotted that nosy neighbor peeking out from behind a tree and told her I used this mounting ritual as a training device to ensure the horse wouldn't run off with me in the unlikely event I ever fell off. She seemed to buy this.

After bridling Claire and managing to get on her back, I only had one other problem—actually riding her. The first few steps went just fine. Boy, was I feeling terrific, perched up there about ten feet off the ground. But once we hit the asphalt and Claire saw the oncoming traffic, something seemed to upset her.

It all happened so fast. I don't know if it was the sound of the garbage truck or that pesky weed whacker that did it. Claire started going backwards in big circles in the middle of the two-lane street; meanwhile, she seemed to be lowering her back legs—or was it raising her front legs? Whichever it was, she was now whirling around and around. I pulled on the reins and yelled, "Whoa!" which I now admit might have scared her and made her back up even more.

In what seemed like seconds there were cars backed up in both directions. At least thirty of my neighbors were jumping around yelling, panic all over their faces. (Most of those people I didn't even know lived on my street until this event.) There I was, stuck on top of this swirling, gigantic, frantic animal, with every car in Sacramento waiting and all these nosy neighbors watching.

"What's the matter, people? Haven't you ever seen a horse before? Good God, go back in your houses and leave me to my profession, here!" If only I had had some sort of lasso. I could have starting circling it to show them I knew a thing or two about country living.

But the neighbors wouldn't go back in their houses, and I could hear sirens approaching and helicopters circling overhead. At this point my natural horsemanship instincts must have kicked in because without even knowing it, I decided to dismount. Subconsciously, I cued Claire to fling up her back legs simultaneously, kind of like a rodeo horse. This may have looked like a surprise to me, but it was all in the plan. It was all for the sake of the neighbors, so they could feel helpful by bringing me ice packs, pillows and blankets, Band-Aids, and stuff like that after I came to my sudden rest on the side of the road. Besides, I didn't want them to feel bad that they didn't have a horse themselves. Jealousy can be a big problem, after all.

When things had settled down a bit, I decided it would be best if I kept things calm and simply returned Claire to her pasture. I knew people were still spying on us. Clearly, it was time to mellow out with a basic, calming horsey chore. Like feeding. I'm no dummy; I knew this involved hay. Unfortunately, we were out.

Since the truck used so much gas, I thought I might as well just take the BMW to the feed store. (And a good, thrifty idea that was, which explains why even now there's often a bale of hay sticking out of the trunk.) But never mind that. I knew how to hoist that bale into a wheelbarrow and I did it quite handily, I might add. Admiring the twilight sky, I happily wheeled the hay bale down the pasture. "See? I am a pretty good little cowgirl, after all. And my, oh my, what a gorgeous sunset." I remember congratulating myself on my transformation from country club brat to country girl when suddenly the front wheel hit a rut in the grass. I'd been moving pretty fast down the hill, so my momentum had nowhere to take me but up and over the top of the wheelbarrow. I once again landed hard in a fantastic jumble, a mud-luscious, hay-strewn mess. Two hours later I was at the emergency room, having my ribs X-rayed.

Some people, like my daughter, are horse people by nature. Other people have to go through some painful stages of evolution and make the change the hard way. I took the hard way.

A couple of weeks later I thought I'd walk Claire from her pasture to our house by way of Sutter Avenue. The road has no shoulder. Hills block the view of oncoming traffic. Dogs bark ferociously, charging their fences as you walk past. Enough, as I realized once it was too late to turn back, to give horse or person a heart attack.

I did manage to get Claire to the house, where I found a handy place to tie her—the volleyball pole right there on the front lawn. She seemed very nervous. I could tell this by the fact she seemed to stand two feet taller, ears pricked skyward and eyes as big as dinner plates. I also noticed that she seemed to be struggling to break free of her halter. Panic befell me. I called our 4-H leader and asked him to hurry over and help me get her back to her pasture. He was too late.

Claire broke free and took off in a full gallop down Sutter Avenue. She narrowly missed our neighbor Sal as he was pulling into his driveway. All Sal said to me was, "Duffy, get in, we'll follow her." I jumped into his car and he stepped on the gas as we watched—and listened to—my 1,250-pound Thoroughbred ex-racehorse gallop up the middle of the street around a blind curve. Our hearts were thumping to the sound of her ringing hooves, and utter fear clenched me as I imagined the worst. Claire would run head on into a car full of people, killing them and herself.

But our Claire was a lot smarter than I knew. After only living at her pasture two weeks, she knew precisely where it was. She whipped a sharp left, off dangerous Sutter Avenue . . . and onto a road where about fifteen kids play, rain or shine.

Thankfully, galloping hooves on asphalt make for a noisy alarm. Out of the woodwork came some of the best horse people in town, to make a human wall and block Claire from a headlong rush into a pile of children.

By this time Sal and I had caught up. Encircled by people, Claire was standing motionless but pricked with a raging fear. The crowd fell silent. I called Claire's name softly and walked into the circle toward her. She lowered her head and came to me, putting her head against my stomach and in my hands as if to say, "I'm glad I found you."

Claire, and perhaps all horses, cannot be underestimated for her sense of where she is and where she belongs. She wanted to be in the safety of her fenced pasture, not tied up to a volleyball pole on somebody's front lawn. And she knew I didn't understand this so, she took matters into her own hands. After only two weeks as our new "pet," Claire knew me as her keeper amidst a crowd of people in a crazed and frightening scene. She told me she loved me when she put her head in my hands and into my heart. But more importantly, she told me to trust her.

It's been six months since we bought Claire. Now I know there's a lot more to a horse than jumping on and going for a little ride. We moved Claire to a stable, where real horse people help us feed, ride, and care for her. And instead of teaching my daughter a thing or two about horses, she's the one who teaches me. I wait until she gets home from school before I start horsing around. It's the ten-year-old who is the country girl—the natural-born horsewoman who's teaching dear ol' mom how to saddle, bridle, trailer, bathe, and ride a horse.

Perhaps most importantly, my daughter has taught me to trustfully be quiet around horses. I've reined in my crazy-horse dreams of beaches and backyards. Instead, I sit back and marvel at my daughter's gentle, quiet art of loving her horse. Claire follows my daughter around untethered, her forehead against my daughter's back. As a team, both horse and rider are doing beautifully, cantering over jumps in a covered arena. And while at a horse show last week, our horse was calm and gracious as she and my daughter were awarded a blue ribbon. I realized that while it was our first horse show, Claire is an old pro. She took us along for the ride, and we were happy to accompany her.

That fusty old image of spending my fifth decade in life settling into that plush chair, sipping tea, fiddling with charms on my bracelets, and niggling about the dust bunnies on the hardwood? It's long gone—right out the window and into the barn.

DUFFY KELLY

Duffy Kelly is a journalist who lives in Sacramento with her six children. She has produced hundreds of television shows and written hundreds of newspaper articles. Her favorite project is a book she is currently working on which contains inspirational and humorous short stories about her "mistakes" in life, love, and motherhood.

FIRED
up!

I just knew every person behind me in the grocery store checkout line was whispering to a companion, "She's the one they couldn't wait to get rid of over at the television station." I had been rudely fired from my job just days before. Suddenly the man behind me in line looked at me with obvious recognition and said in a loud voice, "You should sue those creeps at the station. You were our favorite and what they've done is just not right."

I was grateful for the support, but I knew he was probably my only cheerleader. Imagine my surprise when every customer in line behind us started clapping and saying things like, "Yeah, you nail those bums!" "Go get 'em, Sue!" Wow! These people didn't think I was a bad employee. They thought I had been treated badly, and they were right. My new grocery-store friends were like salve on a wound. Who would have thought you could go out for some milk and eggs and come home with a whole new attitude as well? I walked a little taller, and my voice was a little stronger.

The week before my career collapsed, the station sent out a crew to shoot some video of my new baby for the evening news. I had been a popular news anchor and health reporter for nearly a decade. Viewers had followed my pregnancy, sending me nice cards and even baby gifts when little Evan arrived. I had my first child when I was a very young twenty-two years old. Now, in a brand-new second marriage, my second child was born as I turned forty. A smiling mom with a beautiful baby boy appeared on the 6:30 P.M. news with a voiceover from my colleague on the anchor desk explaining I would go on maternity leave for a month and a half.

Life was wonderful. I had a man I loved, children I loved, and a job I loved. Then a curious phone call changed my life. "Sue, can you come in and meet with me? We have some things to discuss," said the station general manager. I had been hearing rumors of a shake-up at the station from good friends in the news department. I could not imagine anything involving me since I had a full year left on my current contract.

As I took my seat across from the station manager's desk, I was confident whatever he wanted to talk to me about in the way of change would be minor. "Sue, we're letting you go," he said.

I was stunned. "Why? I have a year left on my contract and the station's research on me has been very positive."

He gave me an answer I could not accept. "Latest research shows viewers aren't interested in health reporting these days." I knew that wasn't true. Something else was behind this, but it took me three tough, stressful years to find out why I was being fired.

In the meantime, I lost a big chunk of income my new husband and I had counted on. He had just come through a dicey financial challenge, but we thought we'd still be okay. My income would help us stabilize. Now the props had been knocked out from under us. No job, new baby, new house. Yikes! That was the practical part of the disaster. The other part was ego and emotion. The story of my being fired made the front page of the newspaper metro section, with the headline "TV Station Wants Anchor Gone in the Worst Way." The piece was actually quite complimentary of me, but if you only read the headline, you might get the impression I was some kind of stink bomb at the station and needed to be booted out the door—or window even—fast.

I was humiliated. I was also lost. News broadcasting meant so much to me. I prided myself on being a journalist committed to high standards. Although I enjoyed anchoring, reporting was my first love. I had worked long hours, bad shifts, and tough assignments and emerged over time as a competent professional, well respected by the viewing public. I loved my colleagues at the station. We were always battling crazy deadlines and trying our best. We honestly cared about serving our community, and we cared about each other, too. I was where I wanted to be and who I wanted to be, but suddenly I was not Sue Pearson, anchor/

reporter. I had an identity crisis on my hands. Who was I anymore? My distress deepened every time I left my house until those wonderful folks at the grocery store lifted that awful feeling of shame and humiliation.

Okay, I said to myself. *I may not be on the air anymore, but I'm still a reporter.* Some investigating was in order. I called my news director at the station. "Pete, can we talk?"

"Sure, but not now. I'm cleaning out my desk. Meet me for lunch tomorrow," Pete said.

Cleaning out his desk? This sounded like he was leaving, but that just couldn't be. This man had led the station to the number-one spot in the market and kept it there for close to twenty years. I couldn't wait to pry some answers from Pete about him and about me.

At lunch the next day, Pete confirmed he was in fact leaving the station for good. The owner of the station had given him an ultimatum, saying, "Either you fire Sue Pearson or I'll fire you."

Pete responded, "Then I guess I'm leaving because there is no legitimate reason for firing her."

I was stunned. "You're leaving because you wouldn't fire me?"

"Well, I would have fired you had there been some real cause, but there wasn't." Pete told me the station owner just wanted me gone. But why?

Suddenly memories were coming back. A year earlier, I had asked for a raise, noting favorable research and the fact my cohost on our morning talk show was pulling down considerably more money even though we had comparable experience and I was assigned more duties. The request reached the station owner, who asked to speak with me. He told me he didn't like my attitude. *Well, gee,* I thought, *any* man *would have used good research and more duties to ask for a raise.* I got a firm "no" along with the "attitude" comment. Turns out the station owner wasn't content with just turning me down. He wanted to run me out. To him I was an uppity broad. Over the course of that year, Pete had been asked repeatedly to fire me but he didn't. Then came the ultimatum. The station's general manager agreed to do the dirty work.

Now it became clear to me that I couldn't just move on without a fight. I was used to reporting on the injustices that befell other people, but now it was my turn to stand up. What had happened to me wasn't just unfair—it was illegal. The U.S. Supreme Court had just issued a ruling that a woman could not be fired while on maternity leave. I was on maternity leave. I had a year left on my contract, which clearly stated I could only be fired for cause—defined pretty much as public behavior that brought great embarrassment to the station. I had always been a good citizen. Nothing like that had ever happened. Now I was over age forty, which added age discrimination to the list of wrongs the station had delivered to me. So I sued.

I wouldn't wish a lawsuit on anyone. It's a very painful process, often full of unpleasant manipulations, pressure tactics, and just plain dirty tricks. I remember one deposition around a very large conference table, the station owner's three attorneys squaring off against me and my one lawyer. The questions were hostile and demeaning. I felt so small and weak. Maybe Goliath was going to win this, with truth and right no match for money and might.

Goliath didn't win. Two weeks before we were set to go to trial, the general manager's secretary produced a kind of diary that revealed the truth and supported my case. The day the trial was supposed to begin, the station owner and I were ordered by the court to sit down in an attempt to settle. I was offered a substantial sum of money. I said no, not if it came with strings attached, like forever remaining silent on the case.

Finally, the station owner made another offer that included the freedom to speak out. It was over. But instead of cheering, I cried. I understood how people felt when they endured long, painful court battles. You can't let go of the hurt until the case is done, so I began finally letting it go.

In the three years it took to let justice be done, I had struggled to hang on to my career. Other stations in town would hire me, but only for short periods of time, and no contract was ever offered. When you bring a lawsuit, no matter how noble the fight, prospective employers figure you are a major troublemaker. I needed a job that would help pull us out of our financial tailspin. Just when I should have been enjoying a precious baby, I was gripped with stress day after day over court proceedings and our personal financial mess.

Then along came a man like the one in the grocery store checkout line. His name was Chris Cochran, and he ran the programming department of our local PBS station. He was looking for someone who could produce and host programs. I applied for the job expecting to be turned down because this was a full-time, benefited position and I was wearing a scarlet L for "litigious." The first thing Chris said to me was, "When is the trial?" I thought, *Here it comes. Another rejection.* I said, "Well, it's supposed to start in a month but I will be able to work."

"That's not why I asked. I want to be there in the front row to see you get justice and that creep get his due."

I was surprised once again and so grateful for his support it made me want to cry.

"Thank you so much, Chris. I'll keep you posted on the date of the trial."

"Good. It will be easy to get hold of me since you'll be seeing me every day. The job is yours if you want it."

A wonderful new door had opened, and I walked through with such gratitude. Chris was disappointed that my case ended in a settlement the day the trial was to start. He really had cleared his calendar so he could attend.

I stayed with the station for several years as a full-time employee, during which time I learned how to produce long-form documentaries. I then had the courage to step out on my own as an independent producer and went on to produce dozens of national programs on health topics and many on environmental issues.

Along the way, I picked up three Emmys and a few other awards. I learned something else too—I learned to let go of some fear. Doors that close are scary. Doors that slam shut are even more terrifying. But if I hadn't pressed onward after being so rudely booted out, I would have missed the most rewarding part of my career.

This year I confronted one more fear. The wonderful people at the station I got fired from decided to hold a reunion. Former employees were coming from all over the country. Some were network stars now, or had climbed up to bigger markets in Los Angeles or New York. Others had moved out of television and into successful new careers. This was truly an impressive group of alums.

When I got the reunion invitation, I called one of my long time friends. "Is the station owner invited?" My friend said that not only had he been invited, he and his wife were definitely going to be there. I cringed, took a deep breath, and accepted the invitation.

My husband and I drove to the event in silence. He knew I must be struggling with what might be ahead. I had not seen the station owner since that last day with the judge fifteen years ago. Were those awful feelings somehow still simmering in my subconscious? Would the feeling of humiliation come back when I saw him? Or would anger and outrage overtake me and spoil the evening? I tried to shake off each twinge of fear.

For someone riddled with last-minute doubts, though, I looked pretty good. I had my blond hair in an upswept do with chandelier earrings to add drama. My little red dress was strapless and draped tightly over my fairly lean frame. Gold high-heeled sandals brought attention to legs that were still my best feature. *So what's the worst that could happen,* I asked myself. Well, you could walk in the door and run right into the station owner.

That's exactly what happened. I had taken my husband's arm when we started through the door and there, just inside, was the man who had made my life so miserable. I looked at him. He looked at me. Nothing! There were no feelings of any kind welling up in me . . . not anger, not shame, not even pride over having fought and won. What a triumph! This man meant nothing to me. I really had moved on, and at this moment I moved past him without saying a word. In the next seconds, my dear old friend who had cohosted with me came up and threw his arms around me. "I want you to know I came here tonight just to see you!"

Everywhere there were friends embracing me and sharing wonderful memories. The station owner sat at a table quietly removed from all this joy, probably wondering why he was being so ignored by the crowd. He never understood or honored this talented and hard-working group. He was not a part of that family then or now. He had made millions upon millions of dollars and mega millions when he sold the station to a big company a few years ago. But who was being showered with love and respect tonight? Of the two of us, I was by far the richer.

Suddenly the music started and my husband was guiding me to the dance floor. As he folded me into his arms, he whispered, "Out of all the good-looking women here tonight, you are the most beautiful." I guess when you've worked on the inside, the outside really glows. This was my night to feel fired up! That Madison Avenue phrase, "You're not getting older, you're getting better," finally is a perfect description of how I feel about myself. I've earned this self-confidence by standing up for my rights and not a passing year or a deepening wrinkle can knock me off this throne of personal glory.

SUE PEARSON ATKINSON

Sue Pearson Atkinson is a journalist with close to thirty years of experience in television news and documentary production. She got her broadcast start in radio at some of the top stations in Los Angeles. She has produced dozens of nationally distributed programs for public television and has been honored with three Emmy awards for her work. She enjoys writing short stories and has been published in several anthologies including *Horse Crazy, Opening the Gifts of Christmas,* and *Horse Healers.* Sue and her neurologist husband live in the foothills of Northern California. Three horses, a dog, and a cat keep them company on their peaceful country property, where five grown children and one grandchild happily visit.

BURNING
desire

Thud. I swear that was the sound my metabolism made the day after I turned forty. It seemed within months of that much-heralded-but-often-feared birthday, my thighs started to thicken, my waist took on inner tube-like proportions, and my arms turned into bat wings. Having always been naturally lean despite an on-again-off-again fitness regimen, I was horrified.

In the past, whenever my jeans left little breathing room, I'd dip into my usual bag of tricks—eating just a salad for dinner or slogging through an extra hour at the gym (assuming I was even going to the gym at that time) to drop a pound or two. Now, instead of seeing instant results, it was as if my metabolism was grinning wickedly at me, taunting me, saying, "Is THIS the best you got??"

I realized I had to up the ante. First, I started reading everything I could about the forty-plus metabolism. I was troubled but not surprised to find that my problem was all very typical. Our metabolism begins to slow in our thirties and then takes sharp downward turns with every subsequent decade. But it didn't mean I had to sit around and watch it happen.

In fact, sitting around was the last thing I could afford to do. I began to significantly increase my exercise. The days of putting on my running shoes every other week were over; now I was hitting the running trail every other day. Forget that simple jog; the idea was to increase the intensity. I learned to do sprints and fartleks and strides. To prevent injury, I studied proper running form so that I could run harder and faster and not get hurt. I bought a heart-rate monitor and dutifully strapped it to my chest on runs; I deciphered target heart rate charts and aimed to stay in the proper zone. I was appropriately befuddled by what is known as vo2max (something about how efficiently your body takes in and uses oxygen) and learned the distinction between aerobic and anaerobic states. At the heart of it all were safety and efficiency: If I was going to be this dedicated, I wanted to see results.

I put all that knowledge to frenetic use. At first, it was all I could do to run eleven-minute miles. Problem was, eleven-minute miles were not jump-starting my metabolism. I worked on getting faster, but my time never budged. I did more speed drills. After months of hard work, a breakthrough: My pace went down to ten, then nine, and finally eight-minute miles. I was beginning to feel like a Kenyan at the finish line. Inspired, I began training for half marathons (13.1 miles) and also mini triathlons (half-mile swim, sixteen-mile bike ride, and three-mile run). So now, not only was I running, I was biking and swimming as well. Using the same plan of attack, I absorbed everything I could about swim strokes and cycling efficiency.

Within a year, I progressed to Olympic-distance triathlons (.9-mile swim, twenty-four-mile bike ride, and six-mile run). Mind you, I was breaking no records. My only goal was to do better the next time. My training stepped up. Some days, I would work out in the morning for an hour and then do another hour in the afternoon. Other days I would train for two hours straight; in fact, doing two sports in a row—an hour of biking followed by an hour of running—began to feel normal. When my hulk of a husband (no stranger to hard workouts himself) couldn't keep up with me, mere mortal that he was, I would sigh, thinking what a fitness lightweight he was.

Through it all, my sister, a nurse, let me know she did not approve. "Why are you working out so much? You're turning into an addict," she'd say. "You're just running away from your issues," or "Are you even dealing with your issues?" and, after getting no reaction to her previous assaults, her Hail Mary: "Your heart is going to enlarge and you're going to drop dead." It didn't matter—I wasn't listening because finally, I was beginning to see results. Things seemed to jiggle less. Cellulite still reigned on my thighs and my stomach was not as flat as I would have liked, but I was ready for the next challenge: my diet.

Considering sugar is one of my favorite food groups, I had a lot to change. I said a heartfelt goodbye to soda and ice cream and said a reasonably warm hello to water, fresh produce, and various forms of protein. I was used to running on an empty stomach, but I soon realized that I could not expect my body to work hard without feeding it properly. It took only one extremely brutal "bonk"—where your body literally runs out of gas—to realize smart eating was necessary. My pantry grew to be stocked with protein bars and gels and powder. Bagels and peanut butter became my breakfast of choice, as did bananas and yogurt. I learned how to eat and drink and gel and hydrate and never skip a beat while doing it on a ride or a run. Judging from the looks of my garage, I certainly looked the part. Amid all the socks, shoes, running visors, and bib numbers from past events were half-filled water bottles, sticky energy-gel wrappers, and half-eaten protein bars; I had arrived.

The defining moment of all my hard work came when I joined a group of friends for the Hood to Coast run. About 200 twelve-person teams run a nonstop relay, from Friday to Sunday, from Oregon's Mount Hood to the Oregon coast, a distance of 260 miles. Each runner is assigned three legs of varying distance and elevation. Both my first and last legs were nice flat six-milers. The middle leg was the one that concerned me—five miles, the first four straight uphill. I was to run it in the middle of the night, at about 4 A.M. I couldn't imagine running at that hour on only about two hours sleep (we were traveling in a van, following our teammates from destination to destination) and I am no fan of hills. Looking at the rising elevation, I could tell that this was not just a hill—it was a monolith.

In the pre-dawn darkness, I strapped my miner's light to my head (the only way I could see the road) and clipped a flashing red warning light to the back of my belt. I started up that hill under some glorious moonlight, putting one foot in front of the other, not looking too far ahead lest I got overwhelmed. Step after step. Mile after mile. Sometimes I would pass runners, other times I'd be passed. It didn't matter. I settled into a rhythm that was comfortable yet challenging, my personal best being what I was really chasing. I knew I could make it up this enormous hill, but I wanted to run this really strong and not let my teammates down.

I reached the summit and began my descent. I forced my legs to run as fast as they could, trying to make up any time I may have lost in my climb. When I crossed that finish line, I was thrilled. It was the longest, hardest hill I had ever run and I was anxious to hear how I had done. I had averaged a nine-minute mile—you would have thought I had won Olympic gold! I was thrilled. It was me versus that mountain, and the mountain had not won.

That's what makes me smile about this whole quest. While my burgeoning thighs may have inspired it, my sense of who I am has bloomed because of it. Ironically, after all this work, my thighs, and the rest of my body, are really not all that different than they were when I first started.

Don't get me wrong. I'm in the best shape I've ever been. In fact, now I stand in front of my mirror and see real muscle under those layers of cellulite. I think it's a smaller layer of cellulite, but I really can't be sure. The fact is, no matter how much exercise or dieting I do, DNA is going to determine to a large extent what my thighs and the rest of me looks like after forty. And between that and gravity, it's an uphill battle to even maintain what I have, let alone change it.

What has left the biggest impact on me has been much more unexpected and satisfying. I have learned just how strong I really am, both physically and mentally. I'm not afraid to push myself, and I'm certainly not afraid of a challenge, whatever it may be. As my body has grown stronger, so has my will. I know I can slug it out with the best of them; I may not win, but I am definitely a contender. And whether it's on the running path or the path of everyday life, there are days I absolutely glide and others where I've got bricks in my shoes. But nothing can stop me, because so far, nothing really has. I guess it was never really about what was looking back at me in the mirror, but rather what was waiting to come out in my spirit.

JENNIFER WHITNEY

Jennifer Whitney is an award-winning television journalist in Sacramento, California. Her passions include health, fitness, and advocating for women and children. She can be seen straggling to the finish line in many different running and biking events in Northern California. She is married with two children.

SHIMMY
and shake

I'm sitting at my computer trying to read the title of this piece, the letters swimming on the screen— "I Love Getting Odder"? Oops. Make that "Older." I try to remember where I left my glasses. In the bedroom? I go upstairs, pause on the landing. Now why did I come up here? When I scratch my head, that's when I find them. My glasses—they're on top of my head.

Yes, middle age can be a series of bad jokes. Bad eyesight, forgetfulness, not to mention a drooping eyelid that reminds me of Columbo (who's that actor—Peter something with an F?) whenever I look at myself in the magnifying mirror.

On the upside, there's sex without birth control. No kiddos at home to complain about leftovers for dinner. And not having to wear pantyhose or blow-dry your hair.

Would I trade middle age for youth? Not a chance. I was a pathologically self-conscious teenager for whom life was a constant source of humiliation. I slouched through high school with my shoulders hunched, schoolbooks hugged to my front like a plate of armor. Every new place had its unwritten rules that everyone knew but me. It was pathetic, really. When I got lost, I was too embarrassed to ask directions. When I walked down the street, I was sure everyone was staring at me because I had on the wrong clothes, the wrong shoes, the wrong haircut, and because I walked like a duck.

When I was fifteen I begged my parents for modeling lessons, which of course they refused, saying it was a ridiculous waste of money. For weeks I practiced walking with a book balanced on my head. I posed the way I thought models posed—one arm bent, my hand floating in front of me, the fingers delicately arranged. Holding that position, I pushed my hips forward, trying to imitate the way those sylph-like creatures slide down the runway, pause, pivot, and then retrace their steps, eyes trained on some invisible vanishing point at the horizon.

When I sprained my pinky finger for the third time ramming it into a door jamb as I tried to pass through, my mother gently suggested that I give it a rest.

Now, in my mid-fifties, I don't worry about how I walk, and I know strangers aren't looking at me—in fact, I'm not even on their radar. As a middle-aged woman with graying hair and a blurring middle, I am wonderfully invisible.

Best of all, I've discovered that I can pretty much do whatever I please because there are no rules. There never were any. Other people are just as clueless as I am.

My first inkling of this came when I was in my twenties. I was at Thanksgiving dinner at my parents' Manhattan apartment. As always in that formidable verbal household with its full contingent of wit and literary talent (my parents were screenwriters, my sister Nora was already a famous journalist, and my sisters Delia and Amy would soon be published novelists), the struggle for airtime at the dinner table was Darwinian. Nora was holding forth about some current issue that I've long since forgotten. What I remember is feeling cowed by how smart everyone else sounded. Consciously I took a step back, out of the competition as ideas zinged back and forth. I wasn't about to expose my ignorance to that crowd.

I thought for sure there was some secret—something they read every day, or maybe something they ate. Later, I asked Nora how in the world she managed to know so darned much.

She laughed, looked me right in the eye and said, "I don't. Haven't you figured it out yet? It doesn't matter how much you know, what matters is how confidently you say it."

It took me at least another decade to realize that she wasn't pulling my leg. And it wasn't until I was well into my forties that I got up the courage to get off the sidelines and start my own writing career. Finally I flat-out didn't care what other people thought. If I turned out not to be as smart or successful as my famous siblings, that was okay. Failing was okay. Failing to try wasn't.

A few weeks ago my daughter Naomi was home from college on a break. She was showing us these African dance moves she'd learned in her dance class. Fists raised, elbows bent, she pulsed her arms together and apart while doing this amazing thing with her hips and behind—a fluid version of a bump-and-grind. Then she kicked her legs, knees to the side, and leaped. It was, as she would say, awesome.

I didn't tell her of course, but I was transported back to when Naomi and her classmates performed the Chicken Dance at a kindergarten dance recital. Hands tucked into her armpits, she flapped her elbows chicken-like, then did a full-body wiggle while she squatted to the ground. Even then she had a great wiggle. As I recall there was some serious twirling at the end.

I asked Naomi if her African dance class was going to give a performance.

"Do this in public?" she said, aghast. Then she told me that in her last class, they'd formed a circle and the instructor invited them to take turns dancing in the center, to express whatever they were feeling.

"Let it all out," he told them. Naomi didn't. Why not, I wanted to know.

She told me she watched as the other young women in her class got out there shimmying and shaking, kicking and leaping. Some of them looked great, and others looked really stupid.

So she stayed on the sidelines and clapped.

I hope that long before my daughter gets to be my age, she'll realize that the sidelines are for sissies. There's only one choice. Dance, and to hell with how you look.

This story was originally printed in the July/August 2003 issue of *More* magazine.

HALLIE EPHRON

Hallie Ephron is mystery writer G. H. Ephron. She shares the nom de plume with coauthor Donald Davidoff. Her latest Dr. Peter Zak mystery is *Delusion*.

GOOD
landings

As I readied my plane for take-off, I had no idea I was heading into an unplanned trip that would transform my life. I yawned. That was the first clue things were going to change in a big way. Having slept most of the weekend, I was confused about why I was still so tired. It was true I was working hard to complete my Ph.D. requirements and had piloted my own plane to some remote areas as part of my academic endeavors. Certainly these things took a lot of energy, but this fatigue was like nothing I had experienced before. Something was wrong.

My husband Mike and I were active, Type A personalities who loved adventure. We married four years ago and packed our time with travel and lots of new experiences. Things like backpacking in the mountains of Aspen, skiing the Colorado ski resorts, boating in the Bahamas, vintage car racing (me) and motorcycle racing (him), catamaran sailing, country swing dancing, motorcycle trips, concerts, mountain biking, soaks in our hot tub beneath the Milky Way, and a zillion dinner parties. There were times I wished I hadn't added a graduate program to our busy lives, but I had started it and I would finish. Maybe I didn't know when or how to quit. It would never occur to me to stop something once I started.

Now, in the middle of my pre-flight check, I began to worry. The airplane was checking out fine, but I wasn't. This tiredness was overwhelming. Can I fly safely this tired? Maybe I had cancer just when I found life rewarding. My mother died from colon cancer at age forty-two.

That my fate would be similar nagged daily. Pushing forty-one, I was close to her age. Yet I was fit and used to being active. What was happening to me? Maybe I had mononucleosis or anemia, and those certainly should be treated. I stopped preflighting and called my doctor, who amazingly had an immediate opening. I buttoned up my plane and worried more all the way to the doctor's office.

After accommodating the nurse's requests for blood pressure, heart rate, pee in a cup, weight, and all the other usual checks, I was left alone in the room. Maybe I would be diagnosed with something that prevented my continuing my graduate studies. In an attempt to shake my negative thinking, I forced myself to think about flying. Some people are afraid to fly, but flying actually calms me. My confidence grew with my flight experience. Naturally, fears interfered with learning sometimes. Turbulence, bad weather, or crosswinds on landing left my palms sweaty. Pilots learn about aircraft performance under a multitude of conditions. Confidence and conquering fear were choices that only came with hard work.

The nurse stuck her head in the door. "Guess what, Christina? You're pregnant. Doctor will be right in."

Forty and pregnant? My silent stare and quivering lips told the nurse this was not happy news. Tears welled up. I didn't know how to react. Mike and I hadn't thought it was possible for us to have children and that was okay with us. Pregnant now? We were too old to begin raising a child. My heart raced as I paced the exam room. So many questions—among them, how would Mike feel about this?

Curiously, my thoughts took me to one of the scariest moments of my life, during what should have been a routine landing. Just as the tower approved me to land, a King Air 90 had overtaken me from above on a high-speed descent to the same airport. I never saw him until he passed seventy-five feet ahead of me from above and set me thrashing violently in the wake turbulence. I maintained control of the aircraft somehow. Dazed, I watched the plane darting in front of me and tried to comprehend what had happened. Suddenly, the copilot of that plane shouted on the radio, "Grand Junction Tower, near miss, near miss." Once the situation had a name, my legs immediately shook with fear. My hands trembled too, as panic flooded through me. I had to take command. *For heaven's sake. Get a grip and don't lose control of the plane. The worst is bloody over.*

I continued the landing pattern. Had I let fear overwhelm me, I wouldn't have regained composure to focus on the task at hand—landing safely. Once I accepted the situation, I relied upon my abilities to think clearly and operate under stress.

The worst emergencies happen when the pilot is overwhelmed by fear. We control fears in order to control the plane. And so I had, but could I do the same now? I was gripped with doubts. *I couldn't be a mother because I could die of cancer early and leave my children as lost and lonely as I felt when my mother died.* I had been afraid to grow up without my mom. Yet, my first bra, my period, first boyfriend, my B.S. degree, my master's, my marriage, and soon my Ph.D. happened anyway. Life *does* go on.

My aviation experience helped me along the way, and the lessons I learned would help me now. Flying taught me that fears are perceptions about our own limitations. Facing them squarely to see what they really are goes against the instinctual urge to look away with eyes shut. But we have to face them in order to diminish their power. Paradoxically, the worst is over the moment we take charge.

Suddenly, an uncanny calm warmed my heart. I took a deep breath and a slow smile crept across my face. I could face these new fears because I knew how to rely on my abilities and land safely. Okay, this new situation was not about flying, but I knew the same principles would apply.

A powerful feeling surged through me, and my inner self took flight on a whole new journey. I gave myself permission: It was okay to be a mother if I wanted. It would mean lots of change starting this very moment. Happiness flooded into my heart as I became aware of my new path.

It fit. How would a child blend into a life that had been full of travel and adventure? Easy: I would include her.

The nurse ushered the doctor in and noticed a 180-degree change in my attitude. I was grinning and waving both of them into the exam room. Whatever had transformed me from the shaky, teary-eyed waif to the smiling, confident mom-to-be, it was time to talk about practical pregnancy management. He covered things like nutrition, morning sickness, fatigue, and the importance of staying healthy. He warned me about stress and, knowing I was a pilot, about flying at high altitudes during this pregnancy.

I assured the doctor I was going to ease up on stress by taking a sabbatical from my doctoral studies, but I wasn't about to give up flying. I have oxygen on board and knew I could keep both baby and me safe aloft.

On my way home I bought a new pilot's logbook to record flight time during the pregnancy. It would be my daughter's first logbook, one that she could continue should she choose to fly. Or it could be a memento that revealed her mother's adventurous spirit. I had been flying high with career and academic goals. Now I would fly just as high with the exciting new job of mother to a precious new soul.

Life unfolds interesting places if you don't have it all nailed down and unmovable. Those irrational fears about dying early and leaving children behind passed. I take good care of myself, teach my children about healthy nutrition and exercise, and live life wholly. When I discovered that I was pregnant again at age forty-three, I cried tears of joy.

We transitioned from having an only child to real family life. Our son was born after another easy, healthy term, with the same calm temperament as his sister. We upgraded our four-passenger plane to a six-place Cessna Stationair—the flying family station wagon. We fly kids, the dog, and camping gear to remote strips in Idaho's backcountry to enjoy the solitude of the wilderness or scoot here and there for new sights and special memories.

My forties have been the best decade of my life so far. I wasn't too old to become a mother or too young to give up my dreams. I could indeed have it all—just one step at a time. I'm a full-time mother, and I also write for aviation magazines plus consult for a back-country flight school. I fly whenever I can: alone, or with the kids and my husband. Mike? He loves being a dad. We all climbed aboard for this amazing journey with children. This life holds all the adventure we want and—from take off to landing—we wouldn't change a thing.

CHRISTINA CHAPMAN

Christina Chapman has priorities clear: family, flying, and fun. After retiring from a successful twenty-three-year private psychotherapy practice, in which she specialized in sport psychology with Olympic athletes, Christina decided to be a mother, fly her plane in the Idaho wilderness, and realize some personal goals. She started writing for several aviation magazines and a few community publications. She attends two writing groups in her hometown and is strengthening the art of fiction for her first aviation adventure novel.

MOM'S
apple pie

We are selling my history. My husband doesn't know this. He thinks it's just a yard sale, to clear out some closets and raise a little cash. I thought so too, until I found the seam ripper and the angel-food cake pan.

It was a Saturday in June with rain coming on, the leaves glowing dim in the underwater light and a pleasant melancholy in the air. Just the day to make tea, put on some country-and-western, and ransack the attic. I was going great guns, performing triage on my winter clothes and ruthlessly condemning books never finished and tapes seldom played. Then, when I unearthed a big round-shouldered box made of marigold-colored plastic, I stopped and sat back. It was my sewing chest, an artifact from a past life.

Inside the chest, in divided trays, were the tools of a woman fifteen years younger than me, and infinitely more domestic. A buttonhole attachment for the sewing machine. Zippers of all shades and lengths, still in their cardboard sleeves. Scraps of white interfacing scalloped with the shapes of long-ago collars; a paper packet of needles, sized and curved for esoteric tasks; clear plastic bobbins wound like tiny bull's eyes with bands of colored thread, one sewing project overlaid on the next. Was I once a woman who made buttonholes and lined collars? Who needed five separate shades of pale blue thread? Who knew how to handle this little scalpel-like seam ripper?

I did. In my twenties, married to someone else, I sewed all my dresses and baked all our bread. I grew sprouts and made yogurt and clipped recipes from *Family Circle*, though I skipped the articles on child rearing. Children were going to come later, but divorce came instead. In my thirties, I had dates instead of babies and did all the things that mothers my age were telling their adolescents not to do: stay up late, play loud music, eat junk food, and run with a bad crowd. It was great.

Now, in my zigzag lifeline, I've traded adolescence for marriage a second time, but I seem to use the telephone more than the stove. We eat a lot of takeout, and if we give a dinner party it's always potluck. I go downstairs, where the dark recesses of the kitchen cupboards echo like the attic. Was I once a woman who needed a cherry pitter and a candy thermometer? Did I really grind cardamom seeds with this mortar and pestle? Did I actually whip a dozen egg whites and fill this angel-food cake pan? What did I cook in the pressure cooker, with its ancient stains and its dried-out rubber seal? And why on earth did I buy, and keep on the shelf so long that my current husband thinks they're meant to be decorative, three jars of dark molasses?

Because I was someone else then, an earlier generation of me. I know that some women visit their mother's kitchens to reminisce about these female tools, the ethnic culture of homemakers. But the generation gap, for me, is more of an abyss. I never knew my grandparents, and I will have no children. My father, widowed years ago, lives back East, and my mother and I weren't close. My friends, numerous and delightful people, have become my family, which makes for a happy present but leaves few links to the past. So I examine the relics of my own history and think about the woman I used to be and trusted that I would be forever.

A few links still hold. I hardly cook and never sew, but I still make pies. Sift the snowy flour, work in the shortening lightly with the fingertips, sprinkle on the ice water, roll and turn and shape the finished dough. I love the growing heap of apple peelings, the bowl of pale crescents tossed with brown sugar and spices, the smell from the oven.

It is not Mom's apple pie. My mother didn't teach me; I taught myself. But I do have a snapshot of her, from long before my birth, with a faint scrawl on the back: "Ginny's first pie, 1939." She is standing on a porch, skinny in a print sundress, and the pie is a meringue. How many women have made how many pies, over how many hundreds of years? I don't know them, and I hardly knew her, but it's a heritage of sorts. I'll take it.

I'll sell the cherry pitter and the pale blue thread, but I'll keep the feel of the work in my hands. Threading a needle and tying off the ends: slide them together, twist, loop, pull the knot taut close to the end, don't waste. The touch of the pie dough coming together, stop kneading just when it forms a ball, still floury but firm. The smell of ironed cotton, and the faint, funny memories of home ec class and the dreaded wraparound skirt with topstitching, five pattern pieces, Easy for Beginners, allow more fabric for one-way design.

Back in the attic, I find a shopping bag stuffed with unbleached muslin curtains, narrow and long. Where were those windows, Atlanta or Walla Walla? Who was I living with then? It occurs to me that they might fit my current kitchen window, still bare for years now for lack of time, if I rework them a little. The yard sale forgotten, I begin to laboriously snip out a hem with nail scissors. Then I remember the seam ripper. After a few tries I have the knack of it again, the feel of the tool in my hand. As I remake the curtains, I can see in them my old skill and my clumsiness, old shortcuts and mistakes. The fabric is dusty but still sound. It should last for years.

DEBORAH DONNELLY

Deborah Donnelly, author of the *Wedding Planner Mysteries,* is a former librarian and a happily healthy breast cancer survivor. She lives actually in Idaho and virtually at *www.deborahdonnelly.org.*

THONG
and dance

On a beautiful June evening in St. Louis, Missouri, I sat with my five-year-old daughter, Lily, at the Municipal Opera of St. Louis, a huge outdoor theater in the middle of Forrest Park, on the edge of the city proper. A mild wind rustled through the leaves of the trees as the orchestra began to warm up, and my body tingled with goose bumps as I remembered how, every summer, from the time I could sit still, my mother took me to "The Muny" to see musicals and ballets, and it always served as a refuge from the materialistic humdrum of my suburban youth. Later, as a professional dancer, I performed at The Muny, and that was almost as magical as being a rapt child in the audience.

As we waited for *Meet Me in St. Louis* to begin, Lily dropped her ice cream cone. When I bent down to clean up the mess, I felt a tap on my shoulder. I looked up, and there, looming before me, was an enormous woman wearing pink spandex pants and a Hawaiian shirt. She shook her head. "S'cuse me, Miss," she said. "Are you aware your underpants are sticking out?"

I took in her pursed lips, her seventies perm, and her bulging, expectant eyes as she waited for me to act. Though she'd surprised me, I looked her square in the eye. "Don't worry about it," I said calmly.

"Well," she boomed back, "I'm not worried, but the people sitting behind you sure are! Y'ought to be ashamed." She strutted away, her mission complete; she had successfully scolded me and, pray God, saved me from my wicked ways. That's when I remembered I was in the land of Budweiser and pork rinds, not back in Los Angeles, home of the rich, famous, and bulimic, where a visible thong is not only acceptable but fashionable.

I looked around, and no one was paying attention either to me or to my underwear, so I returned to my task as Lily, giggling, chanted, "Your underpants are showing. Your underpants are showing . . . " This was my reward for trying to be trendy.

It all started over a year ago at my daughter's preschool. Though some of us mothers were hovering around forty, the majority were in their late twenties to early thirties. Even if we weren't size sixes anymore, we forty-something mothers all had various degrees of style, talent, and grace—along with a tired acceptance that fashion and perk were out of the question at nine o'clock in the morning. The younger moms were different. They bounced in wearing platform clogs—and even dressed down in jeans, they looked stylish in their tight T-shirts. I envied their slim waistlines and narrow hips.

One morning, a toddler tripped and landed on his face, and I watched in awe as his young mother bent down to pick him up. Lily and I were sitting on a nearby bench with a perfect view of her low-riding corduroys dropping still lower, and lower, exposing the prettiest backside of a thong I'd ever seen.

"Look at the pretty flowers, Mommy," Lily said, pointing to the cluster of pink fabric flowers rimming the top of this mom's rear end. I was shocked. Didn't she know her ass was practically hanging out, or did she just assume my daughter was talking about the roses blooming on either side of the bench? I blushed and wondered if I ought to whisper to her to pull up her pants, but then I realized this visible G-string was part of an outfit. It was *designed* to show. My Costco eight-for-ten-dollars briefs felt, suddenly, shoddy.

That night, I couldn't sleep. The thong haunted me. I tried to imagine myself wearing one, and it wasn't a pretty picture. My thong rested on top of hips that spilled over the sides of my trousers. Instead of a long, cello-like waistline, the straps were engulfed between folds of skin that created a murky division between my waist and hips. I tossed and turned, wondering what had happened to the svelte me of twenty years ago, the girl who ran with a fast crowd to Studio 54 in thigh-high boots and mini skirts. On the rare occasion I did dress up these days, when I asked my husband Brian how I looked, he usually said "cute."

Cute? When I was in my twenties, I was a hottie. Now, I'm cute? That's the thanks I get for carrying his child. I turned over again and purposely whacked my husband in the leg.

"What's wrong with you?" he moaned.

"I'm sick of all the pretty moms at Lily's school. I'm sick of their perfect bodies. I'm sick of my body. I don't want to be in my forties; I want to be in my thirties. I want to bend down and have a thong with flowers showing above my perfect ass, too!"

"I don't know what the hell you're rambling on about," he said, turning away. "But if you want your body back, stop eating chocolate and lay off the bread. Now go back to sleep."

I lay there quietly, stunned by my own resentment. Why was wearing a thong important to me anyway? Had living in Hollywood finally reduced my normally lofty values to a mere obsession with how I looked in underpants?

No, it was deeper than that. I longed for a few more years to feel young, cool, and hip—at least between the hours of eight A.M. and nine P.M. I wanted to disguise myself as a young mother, fool myself into believing that I didn't have a fatty lump on my ribcage, that I didn't suffer chronic back pain, that I didn't fatigue halfway through the day because I couldn't keep up with work, grocery shopping, and schlepping my daughter clear across town for the one fabulous dance class in all of Los Angeles.

Though I would never resort to tummy tucks or liposuction, I suddenly understood that Brian, in his sleepy wisdom, was right. So the next morning, I woke up early and, after drinking two glasses of water, I swore off carbs and, in one grand gesture, threw away all of my Hershey's Kisses.

Then—and here's where it gets a little drastic—after being retired from the dance profession for over a decade, I arranged to meet my friend Christina at a jazz class she'd been begging me to go to for months. That first class back, I stood in the rear of the room, clad in baggy workout clothes, and for ninety minutes I stumbled through exercises and dance combinations, praying I was invisible. Shaken out of retirement, soaked with sweat, and thoroughly exhausted, I felt humbled—and at the same time exhilarated.

Dance had always been in my life. It had been my mother's passion, so I began lessons at six years old. By age ten, it was my passion, as well. Amid the rosin dust, steamed mirrors, and smoke from my teacher's ever-burning cigarette, I'd found my home away from home. It wasn't just that life seemed beautiful when balanced on my toes, but dance filled a void. Hard work and discipline replaced endless hours cruising the mall. Learning new steps and perfecting them became more important than getting my ears pierced.

That day, when my middle-aged self stood in the back of that class, surrounded by serious, young dancers, I realized if anything could turn back the clock, this was it. I became a regular. And six months later, when I could see a clear distinction between my hips and waist, I bought my first pair of low-riding pants—and I bought thongs, lots of thongs. I also bought new bras, good ones that lifted and separated what was left of my nursed-out breasts. I added a few colors to my mousy brown hair and got a new "do." This mini transformation took years off my psyche, if not my actual age, and I felt fabulous.

Back in St. Louis, after the musical, Lily and I returned to my father's house, where I rushed to the phone, imagining how Brian would laugh when I told him about my run-in with the thong police.

"I hate to tell you this, honey, especially when you're looking so hot in them," he chuckled, "but according to the *New York Times*, fashionably speaking, thongs are on their way out." *Oh, well*, I thought with a smile, *at least I'm looking hot in them*. And best of all, I was dancing again. To think I owed it all to an inspirational sliver of flowery nylon.

CHERYL MONTELLE

Cheryl Montelle began her career as a dancer who sang in New York, and wound up a mother who writes in Los Angeles. Her self-published collection of short stories and poems, *My Life and Paul McCartney*, was presented through the Los Angeles Poets and Writers Collective at the Los Angeles Festival of Books at UCLA in April 2003 and was featured at the St. Louis Jewish Book Fair in November 2003. Cheryl's work has been published in *Seven Seas Online Magazine, On The Bus, Rattle*, and *Spillway*, with another personal essay forthcoming in *Fresh Yarn*. Cheryl also performs her stories at various venues around Los Angeles, where she lives with her husband, Brian Leatart, and lovely daughter, Lily Rose.

SAVING
face

We are dining at our favorite trattoria, two couples, when my friend Judith, who prides herself on being two days younger than I am, announces, "I'm having work done."

Aware that Judith and her husband have recently moved into a country-club-mode condo, I assume she's refacing her cabinets or removing a wall. But then she looks up from her Penne à la Vodka and does that thing I've seen women do before any reflective surface available to them: Palms down, Judith places her hands under her jaw line and lifts her skin up and back towards her ears. Her face becomes so taut, she reminds me of a parched iguana I once photographed in Cozumel.

"Tell me you're not!" I say. But Judith nods like it's a done deal. She confides that she's already conferred with Aston, Baker & Sherman—"the absolute best!" *You forgot Barnum and Bailey,* I resist tossing in, conjuring up the lioness look of New York society figure Mrs. Wildenstein, the lardy lips of Leona Helmsley, and I can't help but wonder . . . how does Joan Rivers blink?

As Judith's good friend, I offer up a genuine compliment. "You do not need plastic surgery. I think you look terrific, never better!" But she practically ignores me as she scoops the sauce from a tube of pasta. Her mouth full, she mutters something about *our* rapidly approaching "big birthday."

"Fuck you, Judy. That's nearly a year away," I answer, massaging the knot where I'm certain her suede boot has landed.

"Getting ready, that's all."

Judith's mind is made up. Even her husband, whose stomach keeps the dinner table an awkward two feet away, seems nonplused. He has a dour, Archie Bunker approach towards the subject of plastic surgery and likens the extravagance to shelling out for another unnecessary piece of jewelry. His attitude reminds me of my father who, several decades earlier, nixed my mother's campaign to get me my very own nose job as a sweet sixteen present. Mom had one in 1943, when it was not yet fashionable and hardly perfected. At the time, her doctor instructed her to wear a little metal clamp with screws that she'd have to tighten daily to reduce the swelling. My mother's nose, though void of its hump, was left with more ridges than a Ruffles potato chip.

For years, I allowed her the fantasy of envisioning a perfect nose on me, her only daughter. And I would stand totally still while my mother, beaming behind me, held a small, black pocket comb along the bridge of my nose to camouflage my own budding bump and glimpse at what I might, one day, look like. Until my mother made my bump an issue, I hadn't realized it existed. I was in the habit of looking at myself straight on. Profiles were something dark and formless to be sketched in art class. I developed a self-consciousness that manifested itself whenever I knew I was being given sidelong glances. At once, I wanted to flee, to hide my imperfection from whomever the viewer. It was too late to hide from my mother.

I excuse myself to find the ladies room. There's a wait for a stall, and I can't help but view the lady lineup along the sinks: women applying lip-liner, powdering their T-zones, fluffing, primping there's even a flosser or two. This is when it happens. I become claustrophobic, uneasy, smothered by some invisible pressure to measure up. When I look closely, something will always be amiss—out of place, but mostly out of reach. Is it my bump? I admit feeling an aura of déjà vu that causes me to quickly gaze over my shoulder. I remind myself: There is no bump.

I had it hammered out at thirty-two under the advisement of my ENT doctor to improve a nagging sinus condition. I'm told over and over again that while the cast was still on, I suffered a total personality change. I awakened one morning and there I was—Gidget! Overnight, I went from Sandra B. to Sandra Dee. The ski-sloped shape of the plaster provided a false sense of security. I became as perky as a high school cheerleader, using words like *shucks* and *darn.* I wore my hair pulled back in a high ponytail for the very first time, having lost the self-consciousness that had followed me like a pesky twin since the day I turned my head sideways in the mirror and my mother sculpted the make-believe me.

I skulk back to my table feeling bloated, recalling our waiter's little white lie. The one when he said there's hardly any butter in the risotto. I notice how the room has mushroomed with so many young/fit/attractive women. It's as if they've jumped from the frescoes and slithered into the banquettes. Chills invade my scalp. *What if I'm left behind?* Someday I might find myself the only one who decided not to turn back the odometer—the mileage traveled by this multidecaded face.

Judith is not the only one of my friends to go *under the knife,* as my grandmother was fond of saying. How can I forget my childhood friend Paula, who, after marrying an Adonis nineteen years her junior, underwent rhinoplasty, had her eyes done, a chin and neck lift, silicone implants, and was featured on *20/20* as a guinea pig for the latest in laser technology? Growing up, Paula was perpetually premenstrual while I was simply pre-teen. I envied her evening ritual of facial scrubbing and dotting zits with creamy Noxema. While Paula moaned with cramps, I ate a dozen brownies and never got a pimple. Now, over fifty, she gets to look—ten.

Sometimes, I think it's inevitable. Before long, everyone will be nudging all contours north while I allow gravity to slide and seek the opposite pole. My husband watches me pull in my chair. He's giving off that beam, in the wake of which, if I catch it just right, I can see myself as he sees me: straight on, smooth, almost perfect—owning the face I'd want to keep.

SANDE BORITZ BERGER

After two decades as a video/film producer, Sande Boritz Berger returned to her first passion, writing both fiction and nonfiction, full time. Her short stories and essays have appeared in many collections, including *Every Woman Has a Story, Ophelia's Mom,* and *Aunties: Thirty-Five Writers Celebrate Their Other Mother.* She is a frequent contributor to the anthology series *Cup of Comfort* by Adams Media. She lives in Manhattan and Bridgehampton with her husband—the one who likes her face just the way it is!

LILA

con brio

The news of Lila Schumacher Stone Kabelyev-ski's death came to me in the midst of my midlife crisis. At least that's where everyone told me I was when I said that I was thinking about leaving the legal profession after nineteen miserable years. I hadn't been practicing law so much as enduring it, and I couldn't do it any more.

I did some quick calculations. Lila must have been nearly a hundred years old. I hadn't thought about her for a long time, but as I recalled all the stories I'd heard about her and what I knew about her myself, I realized for the first time what a truly remarkable person she'd been.

Lila wouldn't have considered herself a feminist, and yet the example she set by the way she lived was all about empowerment. What would Lila do, I asked myself, intending no disrespect to those whose bumper stickers posed a similar question to a higher figure of authority. She'd walk away, I decided. She'd move on. She would never think that at forty-three it was too late to change her path in life.

Lila Stone blew into my hometown on a blustery day in March of 1942. She carried with her a pasty, thin-lipped six-year-old, her son Roger, and an equally pasty and thin-lipped older woman, her mother, Mrs. Schumacher. It was as if all the life force of the three of them had been concentrated in Lila. She radiated energy and passion. Her jet-black hair was rich and wavy, her dark eyes gleamed with untold secrets.

No, they didn't have any relations here, Lila told the owner of The Elms Motel on the edge of town, where they asked to rent a room for a week while they found a suitable house. And no, they didn't know anyone who lived here. They just thought it looked like a lovely place and they had decided to stay.

Well, that was certainly odd, the motel owner told the diner owner, who saw them when they came in to eat their meals punctually at eight, noon, and six every day for a week.

It certainly was, agreed the diner owner, who alerted the bank president that a strange woman *with no husband* had just appeared in town and was talking about buying a house.

The bank president agreed that was strange, and called the sheriff and asked him if there were any outstanding APB's for a dark-haired, actually-quite-attractive-when-you-thought-about-it woman in her thirties traveling alone with a small boy and an older woman. The sheriff checked the records. "Nope, nothing," he said, although he agreed that it was mighty odd indeed. "I'll keep an eye on them," he said with emphasis, as if to say, "That gang won't knock over the bank on *my* watch."

And what about *Mr. Stone*? The motel owner and diner owner and the bank president all asked the same question, with the same inflection. When would he be joining them? Lila deflected their questions deftly for some time, but then suddenly announced to Rosie the waitress one evening over meatloaf and mashed potatoes, "He *won't* be joining us. I've divorced him."

There was a collective gasp heard around the town. Not a single person who lived there had ever been divorced. People had *heard* of divorce; movie stars and rich people got them all the time. But not real people. Not anyone anybody knew. Lila might as well have sewn a red "D" on her twin set.

If Lila felt the disapproval in the air, she ignored it. And true to her word, within a week she had purchased a white clapboard house on the east side of town. It had been sitting empty a good while, the previous owner having tacked on rooms and porches without being discouraged by his lack of tools or skill. As a result, you walked in the front door and found yourself in the dining room, took a sharp left and down three very precipitous steps into the living room, two steps up through a narrow opening in the corner into the kitchen, and only through that room up the stairs to the bedrooms and bath.

Lila put her mother to work scrubbing the front porch and repainting the steps a bold red. The neighbors watched as Mrs. Schumacher spent April and May digging and planting and wielding a lethal pair of hedge clippers, slowing transforming the overgrown lawn into a charming garden.

Lila joined the church choir and sang every Sunday in a husky, off-kilter alto, head high, hymnal held straight out before her with her hands gracefully aligned along the spine, as if she were a famous mezzo-soprano in concert.

Roger, meanwhile, spent his days on the front porch purposefully scuffing the toes of his new Buster Browns by dragging them over the floorboards, ignoring all overtures from the neighborhood children to "come out and play." He was there, staring balefully into the street, the day the Beverly Music Store van pulled up in front of the house and unloaded a glossy black upright piano.

Soon a discreet sign appeared in the front window: Piano Lessons Given. The grammar school music teacher was outraged. It was *always* understood, she fumed to anyone who would listen, that *she* gave the beginner piano lessons in town, and the older students went to the church organist. There was no need for three piano teachers in a town this size, simply *no need*.

While most people were sympathetic, and agreed with her actually, when it was discovered that Mrs. Stone was charging fifty cents less per half-hour lesson than either the music teacher or the church organist, it wasn't long before a regular stream of would-be pianists were lugging their music satchels up Mrs. Stone's red steps, despite the long-time "understanding."

By the time I started making my way up the red steps to her door, Lila Stone had been giving piano lessons for nearly thirty years and was probably touching sixty although her age, like much else about her, remained a mystery.

She had managed to coax and cajole Roger through high school and college. He had actually achieved what some people might consider respectability, having set up a small accounting office on Main Street, where he went each day mainly to escape the din at home—six babies in six years. And since it was generally considered a sign of depravity to have more than two children, he bore the same slightly disreputable aura that dogged his mother.

Mrs. Schumacher still lived with Lila, just slightly grayer and stooped than when she arrived in town. She still worked from the first light of morning, cleaning, cooking, painting, gardening, scrubbing the house from roof to cellar until the floors and furniture shone.

Lila herself continued to live just outside the realm of what was considered acceptable behavior. Every summer, she suspended piano lessons for two months and disappeared, leaving Mrs. Schumacher at home. When she returned, she did her best to sidestep the questions.

Where had she been? *"Out East."*

What did she do there? *"Visit relatives."*

Why didn't Mrs. Schumacher go along? *"Prone to car sickness and hates to travel."*

Eventually the questioners gave up, but the speculation persisted. Maybe she was reconciling with Mr. Stone.

Maybe she was carrying on with another man. No one had any information, but everyone had opinions.

Then one year, Lila stopped them in their tracks. She returned home from her summer jaunt married to a Polish count. At that point, she was probably touching seventy, but she still had an arresting dramatic flair. Her hair remained defiantly jet black and wavy. She hid her sagging neck with ropes of tightly wound beads. She still had a trim pair of calves, which she showed to advantage. Bracelets jangled on her wrists like wind chimes, and the rich, decadent scent of Chanel No. 5 lingered in the room long after she was gone. Her movements were like a dancer's, controlled and graceful. Yes, she was a dynamic woman for her age, but still not the type of person you would expect to show up with a Polish count on her arm.

Questions about how they met and how they came to be married in such a short time were never answered to anyone's satisfaction.

Count Stanislav Kabelyevski became Stan Cable in small-town America, but he lost none of his foreign quality. He looked for all the world like an Irish wolfhound in a suit and tie. He was extraordinarily tall—well over six feet—and his bony, angular body made him seem even taller. He had a massive head covered in iron-gray kinky hair, which he wore exotically long compared to the local style. His jaw formed a perfect rectangle jutting below his compressed lips. In an era in which even my conservative father could be seen in a mint-green leisure suit, the count's tight-fitting black suit, white shirt, and narrow black tie made him seem positively sinister. Despite his massive height, or maybe because of it, he tended to slump and skulk. And he spoke not a single word of English. On the playground at school, the possibility that he might be Dracula, or even Franken-stein, was seriously debated.

I came to dread my piano lessons since the count was always lurking in the house somewhere and had a tendency to appear suddenly and noiselessly in doorways. He never spoke, just stood and stared. His presence may have been oppressive to her students, but Lila remained endlessly upbeat. Even her musical assignments were always brisk, up-tempo numbers in major keys—no mournful dirges for her. She brought out each new piece of music with a flour-ish, like a magician pulling a bouquet of paper flowers out of an empty top hat.

"This is a *wonderful* piece," I remember her telling me, as she placed the music on the piano rack. "You're going to enjoy playing it for a *lifetime*! Let's look at the tempo mark-ing, shall we?" she said, running a muscular index finger over the top of the staff. "'*Con brio*,'" she said, with a lushly rolled "r." "With *gusto*! Now you say it."

"Cone . . . Blee . . O?" I struggled.

"Roll the 'r.' *Con brio*!" she trilled with a matador's flour-ish of her arm. "Try again."

"Cone blee-o," I said again.

She allowed herself a tiny sigh. I could hear the Gar-man twins, on deck in the dining room, snickering. "Good,

good," she said. "We'll work on that. Now let me show you how it should be played—'*con brio.*'"

She adjusted the piano bench back a few inches, poised her hands over the keyboard, wrists tilted upward, closed her eyes and let her head sink to her chest for a good few seconds. Then, just as I was beginning to wonder whether she'd fallen asleep or was seriously ill, she struck the keyboard with immense force. Her head snapped up, her hands flew up from the keys and her whole body seemed to attack the piano. She pounded the treble, she dove into the bass. The piano seat creaked under her shifting hips. Her arms beat out from her sides like frantic wings, her right foot stomped the damper pedal until it gasped.

And then suddenly, she became still. Her fingers were gentle on the keys, coaxing, lingering on the melody with affection.

A sweetly rolled chord, and then again, the attack. Hands, arms, notes flying, speeding to the final frantic end.

She let the last chord linger and drift away before lifting her hand, wrists tilted upwards, off the keys. She let them hover there, closing her eyes again, as if in prayer, then dropped them to her lap as if she had suddenly lost the strength to suspend them. She sat, eyes closed. I peered at her uneasily. Then she opened her eyes, looked at me, all business, and said in her usual voice, "And that is what we call '*con brio!*'"

I ended my lessons with Lila when I graduated from high school, but I still saw her in church singing in the choir when I came home on college breaks. That was how I happened to be there on the day she stood up and told a shocked congregation that she and the count had finally consummated their marriage after some fifteen years. She invited everyone to come and celebrate that event with a renewal of their vows the following Saturday.

It was not the type of announcement that typically followed Reverend Winton's invitation to share. The silence was agonizing. People sat rigid in the pews and tried to avoid eye contact with their neighbors. Even the typically unflappable reverend was speechless.

Not Lila. She made her announcement in a strong voice, looking to the right and left without a trace of embarrassment; and then smiled slightly and nodded at the reverend to let him know she was finished before she sat down.

At the time, I was as uncomfortable as the rest of the congregation, and I went out of my way to avoid her after the service ended. But thinking back on it, I was struck by the irony. Here was the town's would-be scarlet woman, simply because she was divorced in an era before it was common, because she dressed and behaved a bit more flamboyantly than the drab, puritanical women of the town. And now it appeared she had been celibate for most of her life.

She'd been brave, certainly, to set off on her own in the 1940s and start life over in a small town; and she'd been even braver to admit to her divorce. It would have been so easy for her to claim she was a widow—the town would have embraced her despite her eccentricity—but it wouldn't have been honest. She'd had the courage to continue to live life under her own terms, never succumbing to the pressure of small-town opinions about how she should behave. And here she was again, honest, unapologetic, and still celebrating life in her eighties.

It's funny how someone you know for even a brief period can influence you, how the memory of that person can turn up, after many years of forgetting, and make you look at the world differently. Lila Schumacher Stone Kabelyevski came to me in the midst of my midlife crisis and whispered in my ear. She told me to be honest with myself, but answer to no one else. She told me that I should always have the courage to make changes in my life. She told me it was never too late to find happiness and satisfaction. And she told me to always, always live life *con brio*.

JUDITH BARRETT

Judith Barrett is enjoying a second career as a freelance writer and, inspired by Lila, is at work on her first novel.

PEACE
and quiet

I've never liked swimming. It scared me to put my face in the water, and after some mean kids dunked me as a little girl—and I practically drowned—I've never associated swimming with anything positive. By my way of thinking, it was certainly nothing relaxing and enjoyable.

It took my husband's gentle coaxing and eagerness to share efforts toward better fitness, "since we're over fifty," to get me back "into the swim of things." For a very fair price per couple, we obtained a year membership to our local university's pool. Our membership restricted our pool use to certain hours since we were neither students nor faculty members.

Appearing in front of *anyone* in a swimming suit took more guts than I thought I had. However, Bob convinced me that most of those swimming would likely be far older than we were. That turned out to be not the *exact* truth, but the number of people at the pool on most days turned out to be small, and they didn't seem to notice my flabby thighs or my poochy stomach—thank goodness. We also had the blessing of being able to wear our towels until we were only about four feet from the edge of the pool.

Whew.

As the months passed, I gradually got used to the piercing chlorine smell, and soon discovered that I had a favorite lap lane. I have also learned that it's important to get to the locker room early. That way, the minute the lifeguard unlocks the door to the pool area; I can quickly claim my space, easing myself down into the refreshing water.

I felt awkward when I first began the routine, but happily, my "over-fifty" mind and body have gradually remembered the strokes pretty well. It just took a few times to get the coordination back. I was surprised to realize that I was beginning to look forward to those days, and even found the swim to be relaxing. My muscles would get stiff and sore at first, but in time, I noticed that I was starting to firm up a little and my blood pressure was even lower. Swimming was not just something to be tolerated—it was a good thing.

One day in particular stands out in my mind, when I realized how graceful and "soft" Bob's swimming technique was. The water hardly splashed, and his rhythmic strokes were balanced—actually beautiful to watch.

That same day, I felt especially relaxed and savored my time in the water. *"Ahhh, peace and quiet,"* my mind and soul seemed to sigh. The water lapped softly at my ears, not in a bothersome way, but so as to muffle any sounds in the large room. I tried to mimic Bob's grace and almost silent strokes, ruffling the water as little as possible. I glided slowly but purposefully to the end of my lane, then almost smiled to myself, as I turned around to repeat the same stroke back to where I'd begun. My muscles seemed to work together the best they had in years. I was fully aware of the water responding to my motions and enjoying the water's peaceful influence on my serenity.

Bob continued to swim his graceful, quiet strokes, and I relished the muffling effects the water had on the increasing chatter and laughing, which I was beginning to notice as more people came to the pool.

It was nice to see families coming to swim together. Some children feared the water, yet others seemed like little fish; thrilled to be tossed with a *Splash!* into the cool, refreshing liquid, then gleefully dogpaddled to their dad's strong arms for a repeat performance.

I continued swimming my slow easy, quiet strokes as I noticed some college-aged kids come into the pool area. They were more interested in the diving board and being silly with their friends than in any serious swimming.

A sudden, *"Bang!"* the diving board made as it responded to the young man's weight as he jumped up and down startled me so much I choked and sputtered, completely losing my concentration, coordination, and sense of peaceful relaxation.

"B-b-b-bang!" like a cannon, the board repeated, as more students delighted in seeing who could jump out the farthest into the water, or who could leap the highest into the air. Our "peace and quiet" had been broken, and my first instinct was to be angry—selfishly angry.

Once I took a moment to notice the smiles on their faces and hear the laughter, I had to silently reprimand myself for feeling any ire toward the noisy ones. Peace and quiet are lovely at certain times, yet a very serious war with blasting cannons and deadly bombs was going on across the world from us. People were dying to preserve our safety and freedom.

The reality of it smacked me like a belly buster: We all needed to seize the day and cherish our friends and loved ones. We may not get another chance. How could I begrudge the college students for their obvious friendship and good, clean fun? Or how could I grumble under my breath and take more deliberate, angry strokes with my laps, just because the person in the lane next to me decided to swim wildly and try to do the fancy, splashy turnarounds as he reached the end of his lane? We all had a right to be there. And we all had good, kind motives at heart. "Quiet" is awfully nice, and it feels refreshingly soothing for the stressed-out, middle-aged body and soul. But upon reflection in the waters of that pool, I realized the most important goal to strive for, no matter where we are in our lives, should always be Peace.

LYNNE S. ALBERS

Lynne S. Albers is a former elementary school teacher, and has spent the past twenty years doing volunteer work on behalf of children with special needs and the environment. She has two grown children, Jennifer and Wade. Relatively new to the writing world, Lynne now enjoys having the extra time to relax with her husband of thirty-five years, Bob, and their black lab, Norma; as she writes fiction, nonfiction, and children's books under the inspiration of the desert sky in New Mexico.

TO BE, OR NOT TO BE
. . . *blonde*

Do you secretly desire one of those awesome, talk-show-quality, life-changing makeovers? Oh, I'm not talking about a slight alteration in hairstyle or a new lift to your wardrobe. I'm talking about the kind of change that makes even your own kids stand up and shout, "For goodness sake, who *is* that woman?"

Well, for those of you nodding your heads in affirmation, thanks for understanding. And for those of you who are still comfortable wearing the same Dippity-do look you wore in the sixties, let me take you on a little journey.

Sometimes, a makeover can be triggered by a seemingly innocent remark:

Me: "Honey, do you like my hair this way? Come on, speak up; I won't get mad. Tell me what you think."

My husband Patrick: (Knowing he's been down this slippery slope before, he hedges for a safe, cautious reply.) "You know I like your hairstyle, just as much as I liked it twenty years ago when we first met."

Bingo! Such a finely crafted, innocent statement is practically guaranteed to set the family budget back at least a hundred bucks. In my case, it sent me flying off to a hastily chosen stylist with dreams of a sexy new look. "If I can't be a thin brunette," I told her, "at least let me be a chunky redhead. And while you're at it, let's throw in a layered cut to boot."

The result? Bright orange shaggy hair that took at least five months of consistent recoloring before I was even halfway fit to leave the house. My daughter Tiffany lovingly refers to this period as the "long-lost pumpkin months."

Fast-forward a few years: It was a sunny afternoon, and on impulse, I decided to cut my shoulder-length (now brown) hair much shorter. I wanted to do this because:

A. I was PMS-ing, and

B. The newscaster I was watching on television had a great new bouncy short do.

Suddenly, I felt inspired. "That's my problem in a nutshell," I thought. "I need short hair!" Never mind the fact the newscaster was blonde, much younger, and twenty pounds lighter. I was convinced this new haircut would do for me what it was obviously doing for her.

Wrong!

Enter my husband, innocently getting ready for a business trip. He looked up, unaware he was about to walk into a mine field.

"So, what do you think of my new look?" I asked in desperation.

"Wow, it sure is short!" Patrick replied.

The fight was on! My husband immediately picked up on the subtle clues that I was deeply offended. You know the ones I'm talking about: the sudden, cold shoulder; the uncontrollable crying jag. He bravely attempted to backpedal. "I never said I didn't like your hair. I just said it was short." Then he sheepishly mumbled, "Actually, I think it looks nice."

Too late. He had missed his chance, and I was still mad!

The next day, while Patrick was working out of town, my doorbell rang. As I looked through the glass insert, I saw a florist carrying a beautiful bouquet of flowers, and I began to laugh out loud. Yes, of course, it was sweet. Yes, I know, he meant well. But tell me, wouldn't it have been easier—and certainly much cheaper—to offer a brief compliment (whether or not it was sincere) than to have to say it with flowers later?

Recently, my friend Paula e-mailed to tell me she had cut her hair. I casually mentioned this to Patrick. Still reeling from our little incident, he quickly replied, "Don't expect me to send her flowers."

"Yikes," I told him, "Relax! Why are you so defensive?" My husband looked at me with a shrug, as if I was setting him up, and quickly high-tailed it out of the room.

Soon afterward, while trimming my bangs, I got carried away. (Most of you know how this can happen.) Before I knew it, I had gone from a perky, somewhat overgrown style to a *really* short one.

I approached my husband with caution. "Honey, what do you think of this length?"

Not willing to be duped twice, and too broke to send more flowers, Patrick was ready for me this time. "I love it," he said. "It takes at least sixty years off your face." He smiled, proud of himself for accomplishing the delicate task at hand. Yes, he'd finally done it. He'd successfully jumped through my flaming hoop and with no visible scars to show for his trouble.

Except for one thing—I'm only forty-eight. Just that the heck was "sixty years off your face" supposed to mean, anyway?

But in all honesty, I just didn't have the heart to tell him. How could I tell a man who was grinning from ear to ear that his "compliment" was really an insult? Okay, so I caved. But I had a couple of good reasons for not speaking up. For one, he was leaving in the morning on another business trip; for another, he just looked so darn proud of himself for coming up with it in the first place.

I think I'll wait until he returns. Then, just when he least expects it, I'll read him this story.

I'll visit a salon and daringly go blonde. Hmmmm, I wonder what Patrick would say? After all, flowers would be nice.

CANDY CHAND

Author Candy Chand is admittedly in full-blown midlife crisis. While not writing manuscripts from her home in Rancho Murieta, California, she spends way too much time maintaining her now-platinum-blonde hair, pondering the thought of buying a nifty new sports car, and obsessing about the growing lines under her eyes. Her books are available nationwide.

HAPPINESS
lost and found

Three months after my fortieth birthday
I made my escape. I fled an abusive relationship that I had
moved halfway across the country to be in. Of course, I
didn't *know* it would be abusive. The worst ones are dis-
guised with flowers and endearing words. He didn't hit me;
that would leave a mark that would require an explana-
tion. No, his abuse tore away my self-esteem and shred-
ded my self-confidence, leaving only my psyche battered
and bloody. The final impetus to leave came one morning. I
awoke suddenly with a feeling of inexplicable joy, a happiness so deep and profound that I can still feel it today, years
later. In the next instant came the realization of where I
was and with whom. It plunged me into despondency so
abrupt and so black it was the first and only time in my life
I considered suicide.

But that surge of happiness left a lasting impression.
I wanted to get it back. A friend in whom I had confided all
offered me a place to stay. A new full-time job after three

years of less than part-time work restored my professional self-confidence and gave me financial independence. About eight o'clock on that first night of freedom, my friend crept downstairs to see how I was holding up. She told me later that she expected to find me weeping, and was fully prepared to offer—yet again—her shoulder sponge. Instead, she found music blaring. I may have been dancing. "You know who I feel like?" I grinned from ear to ear. "Nelson Mandela on the day he was released from prison!" She shook her head in dumb amazement.

I wasn't making it up, either. I felt as though my life was just beginning, for real this time. No more of those nasty detours fraught with rose-colored blindness. I had just endured three years with someone whose sole source of entertainment was reducing me to a puddle of quivering jelly, someone who never wanted to leave the house except to go to work or the Kit Kat Lounge. I remembered how he had made me cry on the way to Thanksgiving at a friend's house, a high-school reunion, or my own birthday dinner. It seemed to give him satisfaction to ruin any outing that was important to me. Now, at last, I was on my own and had the money to do whatever I wanted. That kind of liberty doesn't always augur the most sensible decision-making.

For one thing, I still believed I needed a man to feel whole. Before my abusive ex, I'd lived with a man for eleven years. What with roommates in college, I hadn't lived alone since I'd moved out of my parents' house. I felt incomplete, so I went in search of the rest of me.

I placed a personal ad in a local tabloid. The ad was clever and engaging. It proved I could write and that I had a brain, two things my ex had made sure I forgot. I hoped the men who responded would offer similar qualities. I was desperate for someone to do things with. I hadn't been to a concert in years. I hadn't had a vacation in longer—unless you counted freezing in Death Valley, camping in November without a tent. I was never sure my ex wouldn't leave me in some dusty arroyo with a broken ankle, after giving me a slight push. I hated camping. I never had to go camping again. The thought made me smile.

In my ad I stipulated no phone calls—respondents had to write to me. At least I'd make sure they could spell before I committed further. If I was interested, I'd write back and enclose a new photo of me, laughing. That was another thing I was relearning—how to laugh.

When the responses began to pour in, I cleared my desk for triage. For the first time in years I felt adventurous, unfettered, confident. The future seemed bright. If it also contained romance, so much the better. The only way to find out was to jump in. I was excited and nervous as I opened the first letter.

Once I weeded out the incarcerated, the Rush Limbaugh fans, the photocopied form letters, and the twenty-somethings (this was way before Demi and Ashton), that left me with . . . all the rest. I was prepared to meet some men and to have fun, but I wasn't prepared for the carnival freak show that lined up to meet me. Marc wrote his entire life story in his letter—to a complete stranger—about his father's death, his job, his pet birds, and the Greek derivation of the word "hysteria." I placed his letter in the "no" pile, mostly because he looked too much like someone who had annoyed me in college. Ron included not one, but three photographs of himself: one in front of his house, one by the pool, and one by his cars. No again.

And nothing prepared me for the depth of self-delusion these men entertained. From their letters I learned new euphemisms for "bald" and "fat," and after I met some of them I made up a few of my own for "boring" and "repulsive."

The first one I agreed to go out with was Stan. I told my new coworkers about my manhunt. When one asked where I was going on my date, my boss exclaimed with, I thought, a bit too much incredulity, "You have a *date*?" I kept mum after that.

Stan had written a charming letter that won brownie points for suggesting a murder-mystery dinner theater instead of the usual coffee shop. At least if we had nothing to say to one another, there would be plenty to do between eating and play-watching. Unfortunately, while his letter had described his ponytail and height, it neglected to mention his lack of teeth. Sitting across the table from him, I tried not to watch him gum his steak. When a few weeks went by with no further encouragement from me, he wrote again, "I guess I should have waited to get my new dentures back before the date."

Vance showed up with a present he had created: a book cover taped over a blank journal. He had spent the afternoon learning Photoshop so he could combine my photograph with his—wearing a hat or a dead muskrat, I couldn't tell—sitting in a dense forest. The title proclaimed, *Anita and Vance . . . Their True Story! Who'd a Thunk It?* I was already appalled, and I still had a dinner to get through.

I needn't have worried about keeping the conversation going. Vance talked enough for the both of us. He barely took a breath. I'd been to that restaurant many times, but I couldn't for the life of me remember if there was a back exit near the bathroom. An excruciating hour and a half later, Vance gave me my out. "I won't call you," he admonished. "If you want to see me again, you have to call me!"

"Okay," I said as I sprinted to my car.

I spent several evenings talking to Neal on the phone. He was funny and interesting. We arranged to meet at a bistro. Why did I keep agreeing to entire dinners? Why did these men keep sending me photographs that were at least twenty years old?

Neal was a teddy-bear-shaped guy whose form was made all the more rotund by his thick cable-knit sweater. He worked at NASA and was looking forward to retirement in the Santa Cruz Mountains. He was about fifty. Retirement? My life was just *beginning*! An image of fetching his slippers and beer as he settled down to *Monday Night Football* sent a shiver down my spine. Right then, at that point in my life, I wanted a guy who wanted to *do* things—hike, bike, see movies, go to museums, travel to foreign countries, watch live theater, listen to music, and discuss literature—if possible, all at the same time. I had years of deprivation to make up for and I wasn't wasting a second of it on someone who was ready for the long downhill slide into the cemetery. I'd had enough of that with my ex.

Andy scared me off when he said one of his favorite things to do was get a hotel room and enjoy the city. It seemed premature to be booking weekend getaways. Eric described himself as "healthy as a high-desert mustang," which would have been intriguing had he not resembled my grandfather. Over coffee, Nick related, in tortuous detail, how he had moved to San Diego and spent the entire time there depressed and crying. I made my exit after he told me how he paid for his new truck with the welfare checks intended to support his daughter. I went out with Jeremy a couple times, until his peculiar intensity began to unnerve me. If I fell silent for longer than five seconds, he would grip my hand over the table, study my face, and ask, "What's wrong?" Nothing was wrong. He just didn't know me well enough to know that, and read impending disaster into every furrowed brow. I wondered if convents took lapsed Presbyterians.

When it came to popular culture, I was like a feral child who had been raised in a box. My ex never listened to music, and when he decided that he wasn't going to watch television any more, it meant I couldn't watch it either. Byron took pity on me. When I read the name INXS on a CD as "inks," he taped two compilations of rock and roll from the past decade to bring me up to speed. The relationship didn't last—I wasn't hip enough, obviously—but he introduced me to some wonderful music that I love to this day.

Marvin was a tennis-playing Ivy-League grad. On the phone he seemed friendly and upbeat. It wasn't until we met that I learned he was twelve years older than I was, had three kids, and was deep into a midlife crisis. "So, you said you work out," he leered. "Stand up and let's get a look at that bod!" Joel enclosed a photograph of his tuxedoed self, clutching a woman who was obviously his bride—with her face blacked out. Giorgio sent me a sultry picture of himself backlit by a sunny window and wearing something smaller than a Speedo. He enclosed a business card engraved with the motto, "Do one nice thing for yourself every day." I did. I put his letter in the "no" pile. Cole was a folk singer with lanky good looks. We launched his tiny sailboat into the bay one hot summer afternoon. Within a couple hours we had exhausted our mutual interests. Unfortunately, we were becalmed in the broiling heat for another three. If I needed a metaphor for my search, I didn't have to look far.

I was sinking into despair. One more letter that extolled the charms of moonlit walks on the beach, candlelit dinners, and poetry, was going to make me scream. At least Gregg had the creativity to say he liked moonlit *horseback riding*.

Nearly a year after I'd placed my first personal ad, I got a letter that didn't dwell on height or weight, divorces or psychoses, but instead wove a story about how the writer had ended up in California from New Jersey. The letter touched on Eric Dolphy, haiku, peanut butter sandwiches, Stieglitz, kazoos, pottery, and jazz. Here was a music style I'd grown up with. It was signed, "unapologetic punster." My father had loved puns. Inside the envelope was a scrapbook of a life: a membership card to the United States Chess Federation, a postcard of *Baile en Tehuantepec* by Diego Rivera, a schedule for listener-sponsored KPFA 94.1 FM, a snapshot of a sculpture in the middle of the Bonneville Salt Flats, which I thought I alone had seen, and a photograph of a nice-looking man in a bicycle helmet overlooking the San Francisco Bay. I called him up. "Do you have teeth?" I asked.

At our first meeting we talked for three hours, played several games of billiards, and went to dinner. Twice-monthly dates soon became weekly, then nearly daily. Eventually we moved in together.

For the next five years I spent weekends sea-kayaking, listening to live music, hiking, going to plays, and visiting museums and bookstores. My spirits lifted as my perspective widened. We explored abandoned gold mines in the Northwest Territories, collected seashells on the Jersey Shore, listened to Claude "Fiddler" Williams in Kansas City, ate New York pizza in Central Park, and climbed Mount Hood—wearing crampons and carrying ice axes—proving to myself that I had abilities beyond the academic.

The relationship didn't last, but the effect on my self-esteem did. Physical and mental challenges recovered my self-confidence. Companionship and the sheer joy of doing things restored my innate happiness. The search continues, but the desperation is gone. I don't need a man to *complete* me, but to *complement* me. Our personalities and idiosyncrasies should not blend or overpower one another's, but curve together and coexist, like pieces of an Escher puzzle. Today, I am deliciously content—in my work, my solitude, and my life. Never again will anyone be able to inflict on me the kind of psychological abuse perpetrated by my ex. I'm too strong—and happy—for that now.

A. BRONWYN LLEWELLYN

A. Bronwyn Llewellyn has enjoyed a long career in the museum profession, working on dozens of exhibits on such diverse topics as high technology, jazz, garbage, the civil rights movement, honeybees, the Vietnam War, and ancient Chinese astronomy. She holds a bachelor's degree in English and a master's in museum studies. Her books include *The Goddess at Home: Divine Interiors Inspired by Aphrodite, Artemis, Athena, Demeter, Hera, Hestia, and Persephone*; *The Shakespeare Oracle*; and *Blooming Rooms: Decorating with Flowers and Floral Motifs*, with Meera Lester. She is also the editor of two anthologies of true horse stories, *Horse Crazy: Women and the Horses They Love* (Adams Media, 2005) and *Horse Healers: Stories of Courage and Hope* (Adams Media, 2006). She lives in the San Francisco Bay Area.

COLOR ME
happy

"*Are you from* the TV?" the little girl asks innocently as I reach for a box of cereal on the top shelf. I lean down and smile brightly at her precious face. "No, Sugar, I'm not from TV. I live here, just like you." She smiles back, and she and her mother continue on their way.

No, I am not in L.A. Nor am I in New York City. I am grocery shopping on a blustery winter day in small-town Kansas. And strangely enough, that is not the first time that this question has been posed to me.

Am I drop-dead movie-star gorgeous? I don't think so. Do I have a figure like Barbie? Never. Do I have a limousine and a driver? Nope. Have I ever been on *television*? Well, there was that short stint in high school when I was student council president and I talked about the upcoming talent show on local television! Does that count? Probably not. So what is it? What compels children, and sometimes adults, to ask me if I am "somebody"? Well, let me remove my black patent-leather stiletto boots and start at the beginning.

Even as a small child, I could tell I was different from many girls when it came to clothes. When my mother wanted me to wear lacy dresses and Mary Janes, I scoffed and cried and begged her not to make me wear them. I absolutely loved dresses, but there was no way I could put on anything lacy. I preferred the yellow-and-orange Pucci prints with my white go-go boots and hot pink tights, thank you very much.

The more abstract the pattern, the better for this little blond-haired, blue-eyed girl with the cat's-eye glasses. I custom-made my own "costumes," using my Barbie doll's wardrobe as my guide. If there had been any way on Earth for me to fit into those clothes and those tiny little plastic white pumps, I would have so been there!! Barbie's costumes were fabulous and one of a kind. I am not sure I felt particularly fabulous, but I am certain that I felt like one of a kind.

When overalls were all the rage in high school, I was first in line with that fashion disaster. My overalls were bright green and neon yellow. Paired with a Hawaiian shirt and funky sneakers, I was ready. Ready for what, I'm not sure, but if someone had come along looking for a living scarecrow, I would certainly have gotten the job. When the preppy look was in its heyday, oh, I was preppy all right. My preppy look consisted of a bright yellow Fair Isle sweater, red kilt, argyle socks, and Bass Weejuns. I was *not* the typical run-of-the-mill fashionista.

From the time I was thirteen, the world stopped spinning on its axis every month—on the day my *Glamour* magazine arrived in the mail. I would drop everything and read it from cover to cover at least twice the day it came, then again and again until it was so worn it barely resembled paper. I would cut and paste pictures together, mixing and matching different outfits on poster board. I would often tell myself, "This looks *so* much better with this," and rearrange many of the outfits to suit *me*. I'm certain that if anyone else had seen my paper-doll costume cutouts, my subscription would have been canceled and I'd have been banned from the magazine aisle at the grocery store.

Although I knew I loved clothes, I didn't have any "fashion sense." (Maybe you've already figured that out.) One thing I *did* know—I knew what I wanted out of life. I wanted to be a writer and a lawyer, and I wanted to change the world. And in the real world as I knew it, clothes were not really considered that important. Fashion wouldn't change the world, and Barbie was a stupid doll with too much time on her hands. Besides, fashion was for girls who couldn't think of what else to do with their lives. How wrong I was! Little did I know how the love of fashion would not only change my world but the world of many other women I would come in contact with in my lifetime.

One Saturday, my *Glamour* magazine arrived right on schedule; with that issue, my life changed forever. By now it was the fall of 1983, and I was a young married woman. As I turned each page of that magazine, I mentally changed things around in different combinations and yearned to tear it apart and play paper dolls once again. But no, my life had moved into more important realms, like house, husband, children, and endless work.

Changing my life was a simple as turning a page that day. I turned from one fashion spread to the next, and an advertisement caught my eye. A fancy full-page ad for a company that did something called color analysis. "Color analysis?" I said out loud to myself. "What's that?" I sat for a moment looking at that advertisement. I put the magazine down and told myself to just forget about it. I picked it back up. "What would it hurt to call?" As I laid on the bed in my bright golden-yellow sweat suit, the rage of casual attire at the time, I dialed the number. My heart was racing. I felt so drawn to make the call, but that little voice inside of me kept saying, "Don't do it. Don't do it." Thank goodness there was also a different voice working in my brain cells that day, and that voice was saying, *"Do it. And don't waste a minute."*

When a man answered the phone, I almost hung up. He was very polite, explaining that he was the janitor, and could I please call back on Monday. Even in the fashion world most people have Saturdays off, it seems.

Monday morning finally came, and I made that call first thing. Suddenly, law school was no longer an option. Becoming a color specialist was. Color analysis has a scientific basis dating back thousands of years, I learned, so why on earth hadn't I ever heard of it? Perhaps if I had, I wouldn't have wasted so many years looking like I needed analysis—and for more than just color.

I hopped on a plane, and I went to training. I read all kinds of art books, and I learned all I could about color. I learned how wearing the right colors can make you look more fabulous than you ever imagined. The training I received showed me how to fine-tune my own fashion sense in ways that were nothing short of miraculous. The bizarre color combinations and less-than-savvy styles of my misspent youth became nothing more than not-so-fond memories.

I have been blessed to spend many years as a fashion expert, helping other women put themselves together in ways that changed their lives for the better. I speak to students in junior and senior high school about the importance of color and image and the impact it can have on a girl's life. I speak at colleges and universities to young women. I speak to women's clubs and groups. My work is exciting. It is fun. But most of all, it is *glamorous*. It is a dream come true for me to be able to take a woman who doesn't feel so good about herself and change her into a woman to be reckoned with. And it is a dream come true that I experienced that change in myself. This little girl who loved fashion so much was able to transform her passion into a lucrative and life-changing business. I'm paid to shop! What could be better than that?

Story time is over. I'll put my stiletto boots back on now because they are most comfortable to me. You see, I'm all about comfort. Maybe not the comfort you're accustomed to. But maybe your comfort is more about a comfort *zone,*

one that's actually quite uncomfortable when you think about it. When was the last time you felt really fabulous in your own skin? Maybe not recently, and maybe not ever. Take it from a girl who was never complimented about her looks growing up—you *can* be fabulous. Starting from the inside, and starting today. Here are a few things that will change your life right now:

Sheri's Rules for the Rest of Your Life

1. *Watch your language.* Your mother was right—watch what you say. In this case, I am referring to what you tell yourself. Your mind is constantly at work. Is your mind building you up or tearing you down? Think about it. Would you talk to your best friend the way you talk to yourself? If you are constantly beating yourself up, of course you wouldn't! Stop it immediately. Instead, think of five things that are fabulous (or at least tolerable) about yourself and make a mantra of them. "I have beautiful eyes, my heart is warm, I am intelligent, I make people happy, and I have killer legs." You get the picture. If you can't think of one single thing, step away from yourself and look at yourself as a friend might see you. If you have a friend whom you trust, ask her to help you think of five things. When your brain starts talking negatively, repeat the mantra over and over. Trust me, this works.

2. *Compliment others.* Start complimenting women every day. Friends, strangers, your family. Make it a practice to give five sincere compliments every day. You will be

amazed at what a difference you will make in someone's day. And perhaps their life. You had no idea you were so powerful, did you?

3. *No more excuses.* You tell yourself you can't wear that wild and fabulous outfit because you "live in a small town" or you "have nowhere to wear that." Poppycock. You are you. And right now, you live where you live. On any given Sunday in winter, you might see me in my vintage Barbie-doll mink, coming out of church. And guess where I'm headed? Maybe with my family to Applebee's, and then afterwards maybe Wal-Mart. Not to the symphony, or the opera. I have worn my mink to both of those places on occasion. But I am me, regardless of where I am, so I am going to enjoy being me—regardless of where I am. Be daring. Find something that you might not have considered wearing because you were too concerned about what others might think. Put it on. Wear it. And revel in the delight that you are being *you* wherever you are. On that note . . .

4. *Get over yourself!* Most people are so concerned and wrapped up in their own lives that they don't have time to analyze yours. Stop thinking about what others think, and start thinking about what *you* think. And if you are guilty about analyzing others, stop. A fabulous woman has no time for discontent.

5. *Smile.* Simple advice, but it works. Get happy from the inside and be thankful for what you have. You deserve to live your very best life, and you can do that starting today.

Come on, now. Head straight to your closet, and pick out the outfit most likely to get you mistaken for a soap-opera star in your neighborhood grocery store. You've got one hanging in there—I know you do. I'm hoping you've got the fabulous black boots to go with it. See you at the mall, girls—I'll be the one winking at you from the shoe department!

SHERI BELMONICO

Sheri Belmonico is president of Bombshells, Inc., a company that specializes in all things glamorous. Her favorite role is being grandma to two of the cutest little girly girls in the world. In addition, she is a writer, a much-sought-after speaker, a not-so-perfect size six, a fan of delicious chocolate, and a lover of laughter with great friends. She is married and a mother of three and resides in Emporia, Kansas. Her Web site is *www.bombshellsinc.com.*

SUCKER
punch

There are blind dates, and there are blind dates after forty. The guy was a friend of a friend from one of those online dating services that claim to match you with your soul mate. I drove halfway across the state to meet him. And he didn't show up.

Or rather, as I found out when I got home four hours later and read my e-mail, he had shown up, taken one look at me, and fled. At forty-nine, for the first time in my life, I'd been stood up based purely on looks. How could this happen to me? I had sunscreen and used it religiously; I had dogs and ran with them daily; I had lovers fifteen years my junior and did what any red-blooded American woman would do with them as often as they were up to it.

"You are not as fit," the e-mail read, "as you led me to believe." What the hell was he talking about?

I took off all my clothes and looked at myself in a full-length mirror. True, I was no Kate Moss, but then I never had been. I had the hourglass figure men adored—or at least had up until now. What was different? Not my breasts, which were unreasonably perky given their double-D size and the fact that they'd breast-fed three kids. No, I thought, my chest still qualified as my one vanity. I turned to look at my ass. Long the object of admiration of that certain brand of butt man, my ass was as large and round as ever. Nothing unusual there. I turned again and stopped halfway, regarding my length in profile. *Uh-oh.* What was that sticking out? A tummy? A stomach? A *gut?*

I'd never had a stomach. What kept my hourglass figure an hourglass was my trim torso, which served as the critical counterbalance to my wide hips and big bust. Yet as the mirror revealed all too clearly, my formerly trim torso was now better described as *thick.* As in thick waisted. Middle-aged spread. Old-lady lap.

When had this happened? I rifled through the back of my closet in search of The Jeans. The Jeans were at least fifteen years old, no longer fit to wear in public—yet still they served as my ultimate body test. Whenever I had a baby, vacationed in Paris, or fell into Big Mac default mode for too long a stretch, out came The Jeans—the truth-telling device that got me back on track whenever there was a little *too* much of me.

I slipped them on. Fine through the legs, maybe even a little looser than the last time I tried them on. But they wouldn't zip. They wouldn't even come close to zipping. I considered lying down on the floor and pulling up the zipper with pliers, a trick I'd used back in the eighties. I stared at the ungodly flap of flab that stood between me and my Calvins, and thought better of the pliers.

Now I knew what I wanted for my fiftieth birthday: I wanted my abs back.

I considered my options. Aerobics. Pilates. Yoga. Running. Weight training. I'd done it all—and look at me. My body was obviously crying out for something different. Something wild. Something fierce. Something completely out of character.

Joey was a short, well-muscled young boxer whose biceps sported brightly colored tattoos. His friendly air belied the great seriousness with which he approached his work.

"You can do it," he promised. "No problem."

"But I can't diet." I looked around the gym at the skinny young women I knew didn't eat very much, if at all. "I'll do whatever you tell me to do, but I can't starve."

"Eat whatever you want. You'll burn off 1,600 calories in every workout with me."

We started with the Nautilus machines, which I knew all too well. Calves, thighs, back, shoulders—I could do this. Piece of cake. But then Joey stopped in front of a machine I'd never seen before.

"What's this for?"

"Your neck."

"My *neck*? I don't care about my neck. I don't want to look like a fullback, I want to find my belly button again so I can pierce it with a big diamond on my fiftieth birthday."

"Got to have a strong neck to be a boxer," Joey said. "So it don't snap off when you get hit in the face."

Hit in the face. Maybe I should rethink this boxing thing. Joey took me by the shoulders and guided me into a head restraint only Hannibal Lecter could love. Then he placed weights at the ends of it. On his cue I began lifting weights with my neck.

After a couple of sets, he pointed to the stairs. "Come on up to the second floor."

We left the Nautilus machines behind and went up to the aerobics room. It was empty. Joey took two rolls of yellow fabric out of his bag. "I'm gonna wrap your hands now." I stood there while he unfurled the long strips and pulled them around and through my fingers and palms, fastening them around my wrists with the Velcro ties.

"You're good to go." Joey handed me a jump rope. "We'll go three-minute rounds, with a minute of rest in between. Listen for the buzzer."

He pushed a button on the timer and the buzzer went off. My cushioned fingers grasping the handles, I started to jump. And jump. And jump. Jumping rope is like childbirth: When you're doing it, three minutes becomes a *very* long time. Finally the buzzer went off. A minute's rest. Just like that lull between contractions. Three rounds later I was breathing hard and sweating harder.

"Oh, good," Joey said. "You're warmed up. Now let's get started." He showed me the proper way to make a fist, thumb on the outside. He taught me how to squat like a boxer, throw a punch like a boxer, protect my face like a boxer.

"Tuck your chin and stare down through your eyebrows," he told me. "Check yourself in the mirror. Good."

I gazed at myself in the looking glass. Who was that ballsy woman with the tough expression? *Make my day,* I thought, and jabbed at thin air.

From the shadow-boxing rounds we went on to the bag rounds. Joey laced up the big gloves over my wrapped hands. He pointed to a spot slightly higher than my forehead on the heavy bag.

"That's where you want to hit."

I threw a punch at the 180-pound bag.

"Harder."

I hit harder.

"Harder." Joey's voice was tight. "You want to kill him."

I want to kill him, I thought. I jabbed hard with my right, and landed a solid hit—and was thrilled at the resounding *smack!* I felt and heard as I made contact.

"Good." Joey grinned at me. "Three rounds."

I glared at my target spot on the bag, picturing various people's heads there as I jabbed away. *My first husband. My second husband. My next husband.*

After the heavy bag came the speed bag.

"Punch it with the meaty underside of your fist." Joey taught me to listen for the *bum-bum-bum* as the speed bag slapped the board, and then punch again. "There's a rhythm to it. Once you get the hang of it, go as fast as you can."

Like you, I've seen Sly Stallone and Hilary Swank do this in the movies; after three endless rounds I'm here to tell you that it's not as easy as it looks. By the time the final buzzer rang I was whipped. Literally slick with sweat, I headed for the door.

"Not yet. Gotta do our push-ups and leg raises now." As he pulled off my gloves and wraps, Joey reminded me that boxers needed strong core muscles as well as strong limbs.

We started with leg raises, which was just as well. I didn't do push-ups. But I was good at leg raises. I lay down on my back, my arms stretched up above my head. I was ready.

"Raise your arms and legs slowly till they meet in the middle." I complied—and Joey placed a heavy medicine ball in my hands. "Now transfer the ball from your hands to your ankles, and lower your legs and arms down to the floor again."

The dead weight of the ball made boxer's leg raises a torturous cousin to the usual variety. I held on, gritting my teeth. "How many?"

"Just do them until you can't do them any more."

Right. I lost count at thirty; it hurt too much to keep score.

"That's good." Joey rolled the ball away as I lay panting on the floor. "Time for push-ups."

"I don't do push-ups." My voice was nearly a screech.

"Now you do." Joey waited.

"I *can't* do push-ups."

"Yes, you can. Only you'll do them the boxer's way."

I was afraid to ask.

"On your fists." Joey paused. "Three sets of fifteen."

I just laughed. "No way."

"Let's go."

I thought about punching that sweet young boxer's face just as he'd taught me to do earlier that evening. I thought about The Jeans that wouldn't zip. I thought about the big 5-0.

I finished two of the three sets.

That was months ago. I've got my abs back, but that's the least of it. Now I make it through sixteen rounds—throwing combinations, doing three sets of push-ups on my fists, working out right alongside Joey's fighters, all testosterone-driven males in their late teens and early twenties training to go pro. At our last workout, one of Joey's skinny young clients came up from the first floor to consult with him.

"Are you going to teach her to box, too?" I asked him after she went back downstairs.

"Are you kidding? She could never do this." Joey grinned at me. "She's not tough like you."

I smiled. *Not like tough like me.*

Hello, 5-0.

PAULA MUNIER

An editor by day and writer by night, Paula Munier is the author of *On Being Blonde*. Her short stories have appeared in such anthologies as *HerStory*, *Angel Over My Shoulder*, *Tour of Duty*, and *Horse Crazy*. She lives with her family, two dogs, and a cat, in Massachusetts. Boxing keeps her sane *and* fit.

A ROSE BY
any other name

"*Can you spell* that for me again?" Not a surprising request for a last name that had four syllables, but this was a question I knew I could get used to.

I had recently remarried at the age of fifty-three and gone through the grueling process of changing my name—for the third time. No, I am not a thrice-married lady. I just have this thing about names. Let me give you some background . . .

Remember the scene from the movie *My Big Fat Greek Wedding*, where the main character has to explain the origins of her ethnic name to her in-laws-to-be? That could have been a snapshot of my life. Having moved us from the immigrant-laden San Francisco Bay Area to a small town in Indiana, my parents had me discovering Americans who somehow lumped Greeks in with other darker-haired peoples, just as in the movie. Was it close to being Armenian? Italian? Guatemalan? Did the country still exist?

I grew up in a bubble, where my parents fiercely tried to maintain an ethnic-rooted existence in a very apple-pie locale. We were blessed with a short Greek name, not difficult to pronounce but nonetheless foreign to the Midwestern ear. It was on our occasional visits to the nearest Greek Orthodox church—some sixty miles away in the state capital—that I realized that there were others like us. But it was only after a college year abroad in the Old Country, my second after a family trip when I was an adolescent, that I felt at ease with my "Greekness."

With no Greek boys in existence in our Indiana town, my parents decided that it would be impractical for me to date or even socialize very much with members of the opposite sex. They reluctantly consented to permit me that rite of passage when I turned eighteen, but even after it was granted, one or two dates with a boy would have my father asking in what religion we could possibly raise our children. Then my dad would look at me and say, "Dena Anastasia *Simmons*?" "Dena *Jones*?" What was the point in trying to develop my socio-romantic skills when I knew what automatically would ensue on the home front?

As a result, I gave up on dating for as long as I was still living within the bosom of my family. Instead, I decided to save the real-life experiences for when I gained my freedom. And freedom to return to the Bay Area was what I yearned for. Graduation from college was set for the summer of '73, but even though I had reached legal adult status, I would never have dreamed of giving my parents ultimatums about moving out. I just "worked" on them until they realized that it was a lost cause to try to keep me in Indiana.

As a member of a generation in which few women struck out on their own, my mother silently applauded my efforts. It was she who grabbed the newspaper classifieds and pointed out employment agencies she thought might aid me in my quest to find jobs in San Francisco. And after graduation, it was with my mother that I made my foggy San Francisco summer visit. We plopped ourselves down in elegant surroundings of the St. Francis Hotel lobby, and she listened as I dropped dime after dime into a pay phone, looking for any job I could get.

That was the beginning of my adult life. Satisfied that I was relatively safe (renting a room from an elderly Greek woman for $80 per month) and employed (working in an administrative position having nothing to do with my studies in college), my parents returned to Indiana, waiting for my letters and phone calls to keep them posted.

In time, it was assumed, I would date the boys with the satisfying-sounding names. But as I approached age thirty and my biological clock began ticking loudly, no life mate of Greek origin seemed to magically appear.

"How do you pronounce that again? Kore—ah—MEN—tis?" The clerk is now bravely trying to master both written and verbal forms of my newly acquired moniker. "No, there's no "n" in it. It's Koor—ah—MEH—tiss," I say, in my schoolteacher tone. She smiles and this time gets it right.

I did eventually marry, but not to a Greek after all. My heart was captured by a dark-haired, deep-voiced man of Italian-Portuguese descent. Since he liked my family and my family took to him, it seemed it would work. My last name was ethnic enough for my parents, taking into account that I was soon approaching spinster status, and within a few years our daughter was given a name (Sophia) that was just Old Country enough and suited both our backgrounds.

With one foot in the old world (many of us having admired our mothers' traditional, doting wifely roles) and the voice of *Cosmo*'s Helen Gurley Brown ushering in the "me" generation of liberated women, I believe that many of us stayed in our marriages longer than women starting out in marriage would now.

I tried desperately to understand my husband all those years and found it to be oppressively one-sided—to the point of seeing parts of myself chip away over time, even the part of me that once reveled in being Greek, despite having given up my Greek name long ago. I had become a lock-stock-and-barrel extension of another person in many ways without even realizing it. I was now the mother of an almost-grown daughter. I was turning fifty, and I faced the prospect of another twenty years just like the past twenty. Like many other women my age, I was saying to myself, "Is this all there is to look forward to?" Of course, the reasons for my marital unhappiness go much deeper, but suffice it to say that I had hit a proverbial wall that I found I could no longer scale. It was time to decide on which side I could imagine myself until old age.

Again, I chose the uncertainty and exhilaration of freedom. And again, I moved back to my beloved San Francisco.

This time, though, I was accompanied by my seventeen-year-old daughter, nearly finished with her high school studies but determined to gain independence herself just as soon as she could. Our daughter had witnessed some of the ugliness inherent in a relationship consisting of two unhappy people staying together for the sake of appearances. To this day, I am sure it took its toll on her. I will never forget, however, the words she spoke to me the night I told her the marriage was over. "You know, Mom—all those years you told me you were strong for staying in your marriage. I think you are showing more strength by leaving."

I was to find that my family would welcome my daughter and me with open arms. I was secretly relieved that my mother, who had passed away about seven years earlier, was not on hand to try to help me through this as I knew she would take it upon herself to do. I also realized that had my mother still been there, she would have encouraged me to reconsider my commitment to my marriage. It may sound corny, but I am a strong believer that things happen in life at just the right times. And perhaps I have led a somewhat "charmed" existence, but I have never regretted my life-changing decisions, no matter when I made them.

I changed my name back to its Greek origins and happily remembered my old signature when brandishing a pen (name change number two).

It was within a month or so of my move back to the Bay Area that I was invited to a family party, held by some friends from my Greek-American past. A girlfriend who had served as the maid of honor at my wedding all those years ago was turning fifty. Through the years, my girlfriend and I had exchanged letters, keeping one another posted of major life events. And from time to time I would chat with her and inquire about her handsome brother, George, chronicling his relationships and noting that he had never married.

Also occasionally, we would be visiting the Bay Area and I would see George at Greek weddings, Easter picnics, or church food festivals, leading the Greek dance lines with machismo and style unmatched by anyone on the dance floor. Yearning for those early days of ethnic belonging, I would dive into the dance line next to him to learn the dance variations from an expert.

George represented all that I had dreamed about as a girl and then put aside hope for as I waited for what would happen next. He was intellectually curious, wonderfully social, sensitive, and funny—in addition to being Greek. But George and I had met years ago, when I was already dating the person who would turn out to be my husband and at a time when I only had eyes for feathering my nest. It wasn't until now that I realized what a great guy he was and probably always had been. When I really thought about it, George had been there for most of my major life events: he was an usher in my wedding, attended my daughter's christening, and acted as pall-bearer at both my parents' funerals.

I was determined to get to know him better—easy enough, as he was helping to host the family party—and this time I had nothing to lose. I was free to experience people, places, and activities that brought me joy at last.

From the moment I walked into the house the day of the party, I realized that I had George's attention. While he was busily acting as a gracious host, I rediscovered my lost talent for flirting—something I had not had any reason to practice since my twenties.

What struck me, however, was the first probing question George asked me almost immediately after I arrived. As he stood over the sink, washing lettuce, he asked, "So, do you think there's a chance of reconciliation?"

I was taken aback by the bluntness and immediacy of the question, but I regarded it as serious interest, not having seen George since his father's funeral a few years back.

As the party ended, George walked me to my car, his sisters and assorted cousins watching us while immersed in their own long, Greek goodbyes at the doorstep. He said he wanted to see me again and I said that it would be "heavenly." Heavenly? When had I ever expressed myself that way before?

Within a few days, he called and said he would pick me up for breakfast at his favorite hole-in-the-wall eatery. When he drove up on a magnificent motorcycle, I managed to suppress all attempts to play coy and emerged from my brothers' house to greet him. Within a few minutes, he was in the house and we were making small talk. I nervously blurted that I was attempting to go through twenty years of my brothers' accumulated bachelor dirt in the house to assure him that this was *not* the way I personally lived. He laughed softly as he looked down at me. Soon, one of my diatribes was interrupted by a soft, languorous kiss obviously laden with pent-up desire.

I pictured myself in a Doris Day/Rock Hudson movie. The kiss made my knees weak. And I even recall lifting one foot behind me just like Doris. It was at that moment that George admitted that he had been waiting to kiss me for twenty-five years.

And so my story ends with contentment. This newfound peace, however, is not a result of finally having acquired a married Greek name at last. It is there because I have been given my soul mate.

"What kind of name is that?" the clerk asks, as she hands me my purchase.

Although I answer regarding its ethnic origin, all I knew was that this name felt pretty damned good.

DENA KOUREMETIS

A motivational sales trainer, columnist, and author in the real-estate industry, for the past ten years Dena Kouremetis has also been a contributor to women's Web sites on parenting, mother-daughter relationships, and grief-loss recovery. She lives with her husband in the San Francisco Bay Area and continues in her desire to inspire and provoke thought with her occasional essays on the glorious passage of time as well as what it can teach us.

THE ART OF
living

I slashed with wild abandon. The crimson stain spread—but not far enough. I drove my knife to its pristine white target, again and again. *So this is what my life's come to,* I thought. *At fifty-five, I've become a killer painter.*

I've hung my work in galleries and restaurants all over Los Angeles and San Francisco, as well as in Sacramento, California's capital, and my adopted hometown of some thirty years. But it's been a long journey to get to the place where I can allow myself to pursue a career in art.

To use a weird old expression, art has always been the elephant in the room for me—seen but not talked about. I've always loved seeing it, touching it, appreciating it, even coveting it. But it's taken me nearly six decades to realize that of the many careers I've enjoyed—from journalism to arts management, television news to public relations—being an artist is the one that's most fulfilling, joyful, and truly me. It's been more of a midlife epiphany than a crisis: discovering that the ability to succeed and make money doing something is not the same as loving to do that thing.

Although my love for art was born in the great American Midwest—as was I, in 1950—it took my migrating to the West to free my spirit and hands to begin to actually make some.

I had started my journey in college, when I escaped my tiny hometown of LaSalle, Illinois (population 10,000), lamming out for the gallery and museum action of Chicago. There, I was able to explore "real" art as I pursued a bachelor's degree in journalism, then a career in arts management.

When I moved to California in 1976, the initial goal was to try my hand at television news. I spent two years as a reporter/anchor at the local NBC outlet in Sacramento, doing what I'd imagined would be my dream job. But I soon met and married the man of my dreams and left the self-absorbed world of television, mainly so our work and home schedules would match. It wasn't until I turned thirty-five that I began to realize my real calling, when I sat in on a life painting course at Sacramento State University.

As I leaned my seven-months-pregnant belly in the general proximity of a three-by-three-foot piece of gessoed craft paper on the floor—my brush going as fast as it could since I knew the model would change her position in only five minutes—I heard the teacher, a renowned painter himself, tear my previous work to shreds. His comments weren't unkind, simply indicative of someone who thought I needed to learn, to "see like an artist."

I guess by the end of the class I was seeing twenty-twenty. After my husband Ed urged me to frame twenty-five of those quickly rendered figure paintings, a local restaurant asked to display them. It was my first solo show—and to my astonishment, it sold out. It was an auspicious beginning. But if I'd thought moving out West was a journey, I hadn't seen nothin' yet.

I'd always prided myself on making my own way, from working Saturdays during high school, part-time all through college to earn my tuition, to vying back and forth with Ed over which one of us was earning more money that year.

The money I began to make selling my paintings was hardly enough to live on. My output wasn't huge, either, since the only time I painted was during our baby's naps. It was Ed's turn to make more that year and for the next several years, while I stayed home with our new daughter. But the more time I spent with Jessica, the more whimsical my art subjects became and the less I needed to have something in front of me to create an intriguing composition.

One piece, called *Grandma Babysits,* came straight from my own childhood memories, by way of the *Twilight Zone.* Against a background of perfectly rounded blue trees, a garden of skulls and two houses (one with flames consuming a clock on the mantel and another with a devil peeking out the window), a woman stands screaming, her hands raised as she looks anxiously toward the figure of a young girl stretched out on a couch, floating in the sky.

My own grandmother did babysit for me one New Year's Eve. As I cried my goodbyes, my mother called cheerily, "We'll see you next year!" leaving me to spend the night on Grandma's scratchy mohair couch as an antique clock dinged each hour. I was awake until my parents picked me up in the morning—far sooner than the one-year wait that I'd imagined. My Uncle Rudy, who lived between Grandma's home and ours, dressed up as a devil every Halloween and ran around our house to scare my sister and me. And Grandma Spelich did keep a large garden until she broke a hip at age ninety-one. All of this combined in my brain and came out on the canvas—how, I'll never know. But a winery owner and art collector from San Francisco loved *Grandma Babysits* as much as I did (along with the judges at the State Fair, who gave it top honors) and bought the piece.

That same year, Jessica entered kindergarten and I hit the Big 4-0. I was somehow moved to make a greater contribution to our family bottom line, even though Ed offered to be the sole breadwinner and encouraged me to make art full time. I went to work for the local utility district, hated that, then joined Ed in his growing public relations firm, contenting myself with being a weekend painter at most.

Then in 1998, all hell broke loose. I was diagnosed with breast cancer, a particularly virulent form that involved one lymph node and required one breast to be removed. I suspected I was in for a long haul. Lacking the energy for full-time employment, I began painting in earnest during my recovery.

Faced with the harsh reality that my future was far from guaranteed, I began to appreciate the value of stopping to smell—and paint—the flowers. Since it's difficult to contemplate nature without becoming happier, I felt that these flowers had the power to comfort those who viewed them. I began a series called "Power Flowers" that debuted at a local gallery and quickly became the subject of local magazine and newspaper coverage.

The idea that these paintings were a critical step to healing resonated with many women, and my art was featured in a national PBS special about breast cancer. The power of flowers was everywhere!

I'd like to tell you that cancer is behind me, but it isn't true. The cancer has recurred just about every year—in the liver, the uterus, the brain, the bones, the other breast, the abdomen, the brain again—each time requiring another dose of chemotherapy and/or radiation, each time turning our lives upside down as we deal with side effects and endless doctor and hospital visits.

When our daughter Jessica left for her first year of college, it was as devastating as all my sage women friends had predicted. Even though she hadn't been home that many evenings during her junior and senior years of high school—thanks to a burgeoning acting career—we'd brushed our teeth and washed our faces together and she'd slept in her own bed every night. Being alone during the day wasn't new for me, but it was different knowing Jessica wouldn't be bursting in the door any minute, her beautiful face flushed with the excitement of teenage life. Again, I took solace in making art.

Now, as I wait for her daily phone calls from college instead of her wake-up cries on the baby monitor, I am able to paint for many more hours each day. Ed, who's already been simply the best husband and caretaker anyone could wish for, reminds me daily that my life is mine to live, however I see fit. He's kept his business going at an even stronger pace—and I've been able to at last pursue my dream of a full-time career making art.

I still haven't gotten used to the fact that Jessica is away at school, but my days are different now—in a good way, just as hers are. I get up every morning happy to greet the day. It doesn't matter if I feel nauseous and a bit too tired to lift my head off the pillow. I throw off the quilt, jump (okay, crawl fast) out of bed and smile as I pass my studio/office on the way downstairs for breakfast. Though I know it can be interrupted at any time by medical trials and tribulations, I find myself welcoming each day knowing that I will fill it doing exactly what I want to do.

I now think of myself as an artist and businesswoman, not some housewife who occasionally makes art. I'm introduced to people who recognize my name and are familiar with my work. I'm not just Mrs. Ed. It's all happened gradually, accompanied by tough challenges. But I've come to think of the cancer as a chronic disease that needs maintenance, like diabetes or heart disease—and to think of painting as some of the best medicine.

I've even taken up jewelry design and porcelain sculpture, two things I never thought I could do. My first sculpture was of a semi-nude woman (okay, she wears a thong) seated, fondling her long, curly hair. It's called *Hair Peace* and captures what I feel each time my hair comes back after another session of chemotherapy.

I don't really want to be a poster child for breast cancer and don't make it a habit to link my art to my illness. Not only have I branched out into landscapes, but I find myself drawn to whimsical subjects again. I just finished a trio of clay mouse-head masks for a group show and then let loose with a sculpture I call *Pillocchio*. It's a clay bust of everyone's favorite Disney marionette, complete with jaunty feathered cap and cute little collared shirt. His nose, grown two feet long thanks to his lying, is made of prescription pill bottles I've collected from my pharmacy over the last eight years.

I've realized there's no separating art from illness. It's who I am and what I'm going through that translates into my art. As mature women, we take who we are and go from there. I'm not afraid to let my feelings show in terms of what I create. A killer painter, on the most wanted list at last.

JANE GOLDMAN

Jane Goldman lives, paints, sculpts, and makes jewelry in Northern California. You can visit her Web site and check out her wares at *www.janestones.com*.

A GOOD PAIR OF
boots and a hat

Most women will tell you that there's no better pick-me-up than a little black dress that makes you feel feminine and makes you look great, no matter what the occasion. I subscribed to this theory for years with a carefully cultivated wardrobe that included a variety of little black dresses that would take me anywhere I needed to go. I always had one black dress that screamed sophisticated and demanded respect, one sexy number with a little bare-shoulder action for an evening out, and one summer version with slits up the thigh that hinted of more leg to come. For thirty years, I dutifully updated my wardrobe of little black dresses thinking that not only were they the answer for any invitation, but they would also give me that "come hither" look that makes a woman feel desirable. When I was younger, my little black dress worked like a charm, transforming me into whatever I needed to be.

At forty-two, I discovered that my little black dresses and all their psychological benefits had taken on a completely different shape and color. At forty-two, I indulged my childhood fantasy and started riding horses again. I rode both English and Western and took lessons every week. What a rush it was to gallop with the wind in my hair.

But to my surprise, after only a few months, I found that riding a well-trained horse wasn't enough for me. I needed a bigger challenge. I wanted to train horses and really earn my spurs.

So I started working with trainers and read dozens of horse-training books with an intensity that hadn't burned in me for years. It was like a new awakening. I learned lots about horses, but I learned even more about myself. Horses can size up a human in seconds, and to win their trust and respect, I couldn't fake the confidence game. Deep inside, I became the confident woman I portrayed on the outside. To train these majestic animals, I also had to become a more patient person and learn to reward even the smallest try in my horses. I became a better person and even a better manager, all because of horses. I started taking on unruly horses that others had given up on and retrained them into cooperative and willing mounts. Ultimately, I bought a young, green-broke gelding named Stetson and rode him through the unpredictable bucks and temper tantrums that come with riding young horses.

With my new hobby came a new wardrobe: either skin-tight English riding pants with knee-high boots or tight high-rise jeans with cowboy boots and roweled spurs. When I ride, I almost never have on make-up and my hair is in a disheveled ponytail, sweaty and hidden under a dirty visor. My dress depends on which saddle or horse I'm riding that day, but both outfits have an amazing effect on me and on others.

First of all, equestrian dress turns men on like nothing I've ever experienced. Heads turn, people stare and men walk right up to me at the gas pump, in stores, or while standing in lines—and they start up conversations. This never happens to me when I wear a little black dress. My attire, covered in horsehair, lures men like a siren song. Men come to me with stories about the strong horsewomen that have shaped their lives, and they wax prophetic about their admiration of strong horsewomen. Most long to ride and most want to hear my story. They immediately think I'm a strong, sexy woman who will speak her mind. And low and behold, that's exactly what I am.

The other benefit that took me by surprise was how much taller I walked in boots and spurs. They make me feel confident and proud. I'm now living the cowgirl dream that I had read about for years, but never had the gumption to grab.

Having an outfit that makes you feel powerful and attracts men that like powerful women is a real revelation for me. Now before you start thinking I'm playing some kind of gas station pick-up game, I want to state that I'm very happily married and wouldn't dream of saddling up with one of these men. However, the compliment of a handsome admirer goes a long way in making this woman over forty feel young, sexy, and desirable. Funny thing, even my husband digs my new sweaty equestrian look.

I wouldn't recommend equestrian attire for all women, as it takes a lot of grit and confidence to fill the boots. So for some women, a little black dress is still the best therapy. My point is this. Wearing what attracts the exact type of man I'm interested in makes me feel much sexier than a little black dress that attracts the kind of man I'm not interested in: one who makes small talk and stares at my breasts. I'd rather they stared at my spurs and gave me a big yeehaw!

Interestingly enough, the equestrian dress also attracts a lot of new girlfriends, too. Women stop me and tell me how much they wish they could ride again, or about a dear horse they owned as a child. So for me, the proverbial little black dress now comes in the form of sweat, boots, and spurs. I think this means I'm becoming my own person, but sure enough, the horses will tell me if I'm wrong here.

My new passion for horses has also taught me that sometimes it's the accessory, not the dress that reels in the good times. I get an amazing response when I wear one of my Stetson cowboy hats. Mine are of the Tom Mix persuasion—oversized and bodacious. Wearing a cowboy hat somehow gives people permission to speak to me, and the comments are almost always upbeat and happy. Once in New York, a friend accompanied me on a bar-hopping adventure in my cowboy hat; she said she felt more like a bouncer than a companion. Even back in college, I found a cowboy hat got me a lot more dates than a little black dress.

For me, a cowboy hat is the perfect accessory, because it acts as a magnet to attract fun-loving people.

I'm not the only one who finds a cowboy hat to be the perfect accessory. I have a girlfriend who used to live in Boston, and she also experienced the psychology and lure of a well-positioned Stetson. She is a native of New Jersey—not a Western bone in her body. She's one of those very practical dressers who does not have an eye or a care for fashion. She started wearing a cowboy hat on snowy days out of a strong sense of functionality: it was the best way to keep the wet snow off her hair without getting hat head. She soon learned that her Stetson was a great way to meet fun people. She met two of her best girlfriends and got dozens of dates, just by wearing that cowboy hat on the subway.

So when a friend feels down in the dumps, I challenge her to wear a cowboy hat for a day. I guarantee that it will improve her outlook on life. She may start off the day hiding under the hat, but when the sun sets, she's walking tall again. This crazy therapy works because cowboy hats attract people who are outgoing and upbeat. For a quick pick-me-up, I now choose a cowboy hat over a little black dress. And for you single chicks, I'd challenge your little black dress to my cowboy hat in a game of good-hearted, pick-em-up in any bar across the United States.

The new me may be a bit more rugged, but I still enjoy a dressy evening out with my cowboy partner of twenty-two years. But with age, I'm wiser and now I know that black is not what it's cracked up to be. I think emerald is the new black. Like most of you, I believed for years that the little black dress had to be black—well buck that thinking, sister. Pale-skinned, fair-haired women (like me) look better in eggplant, emerald, or burgundy. It may seem trivial to you, but when your little black dress starts making you feel washed out, you need to adopt a different color and thus a better attitude. I used to own a sophisticated black dress that I wore to three separate funerals in one month. The following month I donated it to the women's shelter—I couldn't stand the funereal feeling and Oreo look I got when I put it on. Black just ain't what it used to be.

It's your choice. You can continue to shop designer stores for the perfect little black dress and spend away, believing it's the answer to your every desire. Or you can accept a challenge from this older and wiser cowgirl to buck the rules and give the old cowboy boots and hat a try. You'll be amazed at your new outlook on life, no matter what your age.

ELLEN REID SMITH

Ellen Reid Smith is an author and marketing consultant who turned her life-long passion for cowgirl history into a motivational line of books called *Cowgirl Smarts, How to Rope a Kick-Ass Life, How to Kick-Ass in Business,* and *Cowgirl Smarts for Kids.* You can find Ellen in Austin, Texas, riding her black-and-white paint horse named Stetson and loving the new life she leads. To read more of Ellen's cowgirl advice, visit her Web site at *www.cowgirlsmarts.com.*

ORPHANED

I stood over my father's form in the hospital bed, a fresh, white sheet pulled up to his chin and tucked neatly under the mattress. Yesterday, I had stood in this same place, momentarily embarrassed by my father's nakedness as he thrashed about in the bed, pulling a crumpled sheet off suddenly, as though he intended to get up and leave.

Indeed, he did leave. He died shortly before midnight. The nurses at the hospital called me at home to see if I wanted to come be with him before they removed his body. And so now I stood here again, wishing for yesterday and another moment, even of embarrassment, because it would have meant he was still alive.

To say his death was expected is to play with the truth. Advanced prostate cancer at age seventy-four leaves little doubt as to the eventual outcome, but when we love someone deeply, we can fool ourselves. *He couldn't be dead, could he? I still need my father.*

The figure before me was pale and still and silent. The bones in his face were sharp and angular. Death had taken the softness of his features away. His essence was gone from this once-sturdy framework of skin and bones. I hoped it was nearby still. I prayed, "Dear Lord, thank you for this man who gave me life and the gift of unconditional love." *Daddy, I will love you and miss you forever.* I cried then and for many days after.

The pain of losing him was as deep and wide and unrelenting as the joy of loving him had been. Grief and joy it seemed were two sides of the same coin when you were lucky enough to be loved and to love in return. But there are different shades of love, and unconditional love is a rare and brilliant treasure. He had given it to me effortlessly. That's how it seemed to me, though he might have argued it wasn't so easy during my teen years.

How will I make my way in this world without the man who inspired me to be brave? It is a question that lingers long after time has wiped away what seemed like endless tears of mourning. Now I'm a grown woman with five children of my own, and I'm an orphan, with no one left in this world who will ever love me no matter what I do or say or become. After all these years as an adult, I suddenly feel like I'm on a high wire without that long balancing bar. There is no net below, and I'm scared. There is no compass, no flashlight, no flint, and no water.

Losing my mother ten years earlier had not been the same. Certainly she loved me, but her love was always delivered cautiously, tentatively, or with a string of conditions. I cried when she died too, but these tears came from anger—at her. She had killed herself from alcoholism. It had taken awhile—most of my years growing up and then some. Curiously, I wasn't angry with her for being a bad person. I was enraged because she had been a good person—warm-hearted, witty, intelligent—and she had wasted it, thrown it away for bottles and bottles of vodka. My father loved her unconditionally, too, and stayed with her through the messy, mucked-up life alcoholics deliver to themselves and everyone around them.

No, I was not an orphan just because both of my parents had died. I was an orphan because that shade of love called "unconditional" was gone forever with my father's passing. While it had once been lifted up by the one person in the world who thought I was perfect, my inner spirit was alone and lonely. I had love around me still, but it was a different shade. I knew that my husband loved me, but there were expectations. I had a home to run, a job with income to help pay the bills, children to keep safe. If I somehow screwed up badly, would he still think I was wonderful? I didn't think so.

My children loved me. But they kind of have to unless you make a truly terrible mistake, and even then they still want to love you. I have loved my children unconditionally, but I doubt they received the message with the steadiness and strength that my father's love delivered to me. Though I believe I have been a good parent—not extraordinary, like my father—I have not matched my father's patience and kindness.

When I was in the trenches raising kids, it seemed egos got to tussling, tempers to flaring, and opportunities for misunderstanding were an ordinary occurrence. We loved each other then and now that they are grown and gone, but steadfast unconditional love is something else. I know it because I've been on the receiving end and can measure its power in my life. My father's gift gave me courage that all things were possible.

Although some days he used the words, my father didn't say he loved me every day. The message came in the little gestures. I remember how it felt for him to wrap his arms around me and then give me sweet little pats on the back. He seemed to genuinely enjoy my company and asked for my opinions about the world. He told me often enough that I was special, and over the course of my childhood I began to believe it. He had a gentle voice and was only once angry with me when he thought I showed bad judgment. I was a teenager; what more can I say?

Even then, I knew that flash of anger came from loving me so much and being scared about my safety. He honored my budding self-reliance and knew that even if I made a mistake, I'd learn something important. He told me I could do anything, be anything, achieve anything I wanted in the world. He was my cheerleader. When I was grown up, he would come to visit and suddenly press a bill in my hand—a twenty, a fifty, or even a hundred—and say, "Shh," like it was a secret I had to keep. He wanted me to have mad money to spend just on myself. He was generous and always kind. He's been gone nine years, but I still miss him every day, with that wee scared voice, *"How will I make my way in the world?"* still lingering. He would smile to know that some wisdom was finally coming to me and that it started in a moment of great doubt.

A year ago I broke my hip. Such an old woman's injury, but it can happen to anyone who trips backwards over a dog and lands on a hard patio! My recovery was painful and long. My husband was wonderful. We live on a small ranch where I can indulge in my life-long love for animals, especially horses. I have two horses, a pony, a dog, and cat that patrols the property for voles. I love them all dearly. My husband said, "Just get better. Quit your job and play with your horses." An appealing idea, but it sounded so self-centered.

At home by myself with very limited mobility, there was a lot of time to just be quiet. It made me uncomfortable to have so little to do and so much time to think. How was I going to spend the rest of my life? It was ponderous and scary question for which I had no answer.

The answer came in the form of a newspaper article about a new organization in my community that paired adult mentors with children in foster care. When I read the description of what volunteers were supposed to do for the foster children—be "a steady, nonjudgmental presence in a child's life . . . a cheerleader, a confidence builder, someone to help a child feel special in the world and believe in themselves and bounce back from traumatic beginnings"—I knew instantly that was what I was meant to do next. My father had taught me all of these things. He was my first mentor. Now I would do the same for someone else. I knew something about children, and I had the time. This was my future.

My little foster girl and I have been on our mentoring journey for a year now. I am teaching her how to ride, and she is becoming quite an equestrian at age nine. Riding isn't just about staying in the saddle; it's so much more. As she works with horses, she is building confidence and self-esteem, learning about patience, leadership, and so much more.

We've been to the zoo and a play. Next month we have tickets for the symphony. Along the way I'm cheering for her and showing her possibilities. It's not hard to believe in her. She is one terrific kid, and I am blessed to have her in my life. During one of our times together she confided that she was worried about the future. Her social worker had told her some important court decisions were coming up soon. There was a lot of uncertainty ahead. She was either going to be reunited with her biological mom or placed for adoption.

I was horrified that any child should have to face such huge question marks about home and family. I asked her what she was most worried about. "I'm scared you and I might not get to keep going if I'm not in foster care anymore."

I was amazed at her answer and impressed with the power of unconditional love. Once delivered, there is a deep yearning to keep it close. She had received it from me, but was she going to have to give it up? She, too, was afraid of being an orphan without that one person who thought she was perfect. I said, "On your next visit with your mother, why don't you ask her how she feels about us continuing our journey? You and I are solid friends, no matter what happens."

A couple of weeks later, as I pulled my car up to the curb outside her foster home, I saw my little girl come flying out the front door and bounce into the front seat next to me. "You seem very happy today."

"I am. I did what you said and asked my mom if she'd let me keep on being your friend no matter what, and she said yes!"

I have an awesome responsibility to this little girl, but it doesn't scare me one bit. As a mature adult I have finally stilled that frightened voice inside of me—*How will I make my way without him?* In filling this little girl's need I find my father's love. It makes me brave again because in giving it away I will always keep it near. Now the strength and comfort of unconditional love will reach someone who desperately needs this steadfast support. This precious child had no choice in how her journey began. I hope the energy I bring to her life will give her wings to dream, courage to love, and inspiration to one day follow a glorious path of her own design.

SUZANNE TOMLINSON

Suzanne holds family, children, home, and horses most dear. Writing and riding are her passions. Among her treasured accomplishments are raising terrific kids into fine adults, mentoring a foster child, and weathering life's challenges in a long-term marriage that just gets better with time.

LETTING GO

"Come on," I hollered, "you don't want to be late for your make-up test." Six forty-five A.M. and the mad dash was again underway to bring up that ailing algebra grade. The teacher's classroom opened at seven for students who needed help, and we had been regulars for weeks.

On the day of his final exam, I answered the phone. It was my son, Jameson. "Mom, I got an 88 on the test." "Congratulations!" I quickly responded. I heard the pause and began to feel his pain through the burning wire. "Mom, I needed an 89 to pass," he quietly uttered. His disappointment rang out loud and clear. My heart sank.

As a professional woman, I'm strong, decisive. When it comes to my son, those traits carry over. For years, I've tried to run his life like a well-oiled machine. Looking back, I see exactly where my controlling tendencies come from. Dedicated as I am to a grueling career, my work was my baby. I knew very little about the other kind. I never sat around in a rocking chair contemplating what it would be like to have a child.

I was so clueless that when I missed a period at the age of thirty-nine, I was certain I had cancer. In reality, birth control had failed me, and I was pregnant. "Not possible," I yelped. But it was true. I was with child. A single career woman, the logical next step for me, I thought, was an abortion.

My doctor, a family friend, asked me to confer with my family first. My mother was a big supporter of my career, and I knew she'd be there for me. But sitting down with her and broaching the subject was extremely uncomfortable. I had no idea about her views on abortion. Somehow, I managed to blurt out the words.

She responded with a silence that seemed to last an eternity. Then, she spoke. "Why an abortion?" she asked. "This might be your last chance to have a child."

I had been reacting without much thinking. Now my mother was pushing me to be thoughtful about this important decision. Through my mother's good sense, I experienced an epiphany.

When I asked myself the hard questions, the answers came back changed. Perhaps I really could have this baby. And then, all of a sudden, having this child felt like the absolutely right thing to do. That gentle nudge from my mom propelled me into action. I ran to the phone and canceled the abortion.

Many months later, when I went into labor, the hospital delivery room was jammed with dozens of my friends. They knew that this baby's biological father, by his own choice, would not be there at this moment. My friends wrapped their love around me; they were my family on this important day. They clapped and smiled and even cried with joy as this new little soul took his first breath. At age forty, I delivered a healthy little boy who became the greatest unexpected gift I could ever have imagined. I had no idea what I had been missing until I saw his sweet face. At that moment, my whole life changed.

I was determined. My son was going to have everything. I continued working, but I made him my priority. If he needed me, I was there. I was so grateful for this child that I undoubtedly became overprotective.

At forty-two, I met the man of my dreams, who embraced my little boy as his own. Two years later, we were married. Now Jameson truly had everything. A mom who would jump over the moon for him and a dad who would do the same.

Jameson attended private school from day one and flourished. With 150 kids on campus, by either calling or looking, I could find my child at the drop of a dime. It was a kindergarten-through-eighth-grade school, and we avoided the headaches you hear about in most middle schools. No gang violence or drug problems, and he stayed with the same small clique of friends all the way through. I was reassured that he was safe.

His eighth-grade graduation was adorable. With a handful of graduating kids, each was featured in a slide show, and one by one they spoke about their years in school and all that they learned.

When Jameson chose to attend a public high school in our neighborhood, I was surprised. I wanted him to go to a near-by private school. *"My child in public school—hmm,"* I pondered. But he was fifteen, and I wanted him to spread his wings. I respected his decision and enrolled him.

Venturing into public school put me on heightened alert. Walking Jameson around his new high school campus, I was nervous. "Your locker is here." I said. "Let's walk the distance to see how far it is to your classrooms." I wondered, "How will he ever do this? How will I ever do this? How will I ever find my son in the massive sea of faces—all 1,800 of them?"

Jameson did well in the weeks and months to follow although there were still nights when he would crawl into bed with me, worried about not having enough friends. When he told me one day that he actually ate lunch alone, I thought, "Who do I call about this?" When he was terrified about "can" the freshmen week—a practice where seniors allegedly grab freshmen and dump them into trash cans—I told him it was a playful rumor and that school officials wouldn't allow it to happen. Inside, I was thinking, "I knew it. I knew this wasn't right for my son." Jameson hung in there. He started making friends, and his grades were good. But ongoing bouts with asthma and related respiratory infections resulted in pneumonia. Unfortunately, Jameson missed three full weeks of school. His dad and I tried repeatedly to contact teachers but to no avail.

His end-of-the-year progress report was dismal. An F in algebra. "How can this be," I asked? "Not my son. Never in a million years." I called the school counselor and finally spoke with the algebra teacher.

"He's missed the work," he said. "But I'm willing to let him come in early to try to catch up." It was a long shot, but . . . "Fair enough," I said. "We'll do whatever we can." With that, the frantic race was on.

Every night was the same. "Jameson, did you do your homework?" I'd inquire. "Show it to me, please." I needed to go through the motions though a lot of good it did. Algebra has never been my friend. I struggled with it when I was in school. All these years later, ask me about "X-Y-Z," and I'll tell you they're symbols you see on the side of frat houses.

Jameson was under pressure to get at least a C in the class. Otherwise, he'd have to attend summer school. Or worse yet, repeat algebra next year as a sophomore instead of taking geometry. The day of his final, I might as well have been waiting for the axe to drop on my neck. Finally, there was Jameson's voice. The teacher had allowed him to use the classroom phone. The 88 he got on his final exam was a strong B. You would have thought I'd won the lottery! I was so relieved I could barely speak.

But with his, "Mom, I needed an 89 to pass," said the axe did fall after all. I paused. My next words were emphatic. "This is not right!" I exclaimed. "Put your teacher on the phone."

The teacher calmly explained his grading process. "Are you asking me to change his grade?" he inquired. What could I say? "Of course not," I replied and hung up. When I saw Jameson that afternoon, he was beside himself, understandably fluctuating between tears and rage. He had worked hard and done well.

I told him how much I admired him for trying. "A lot of good it did," he responded. I tried to let him know that I understood his frustration. "This is all fixable. You'll get another chance in summer school." But he was inconsolable.

I drove home. He stormed into the house, backpack flying, doors slamming. I wanted to spare him any more pain. "Jameson," I said, "we don't have to put up with this for one minute more. I'm calling the private school. You don't have to go back to that damn public school next year."

I reached the administrator that afternoon, and Jameson was scheduled for a visit the next week. Private school would be expensive. I told my stockbroker to liquidate some of the family nest egg. "That's what the money is there for," I insisted. "Emergencies."

When we visited the school, the protective environment was delightful and very appealing to me. It was inviting and friendly—a throwback to the first nine years of Jameson's education.

The administrator was kind and attentive. She assured Jameson that he didn't fail algebra—it was the public school system that failed him. I was happy. But I sensed Jameson was unimpressed. I, on the other hand, knew this was where we belonged all along.

As the summer wore on, Jameson scored some major successes. He and the neighbor's son, Tom, who's in his early twenties, rebuilt a portion of our fence. Jameson earned close to $300, much of which he chose to put into savings. Before we knew it, Jameson was back at his old campus for summer school. His dad found him a great algebra tutor, a retired math teacher, and the two hit it off like an old pea and a young pod. This time, I gladly took a back seat to his studies. It's not exactly like I could help him anyway. My days were more relaxing than they had been in months.

Jameson plowed through piles of homework every night. He spent five hours a day in class and met with his tutor twice a week. He lived and breathed algebra and passed with flying colors. He was grateful for the opportunity to bring up his grade. Jameson was evolving into a different person before my very eyes. I'd look at him and think, "Who is this young man?"

Then came the announcement of the summer. Jameson wanted to give public school another try. He wasn't ready to give up. "Are you certain?" I queried. "Absolutely," he responded. "Wow." I had tried desperately to save Jameson from failing algebra. Now I realized that by doing so, I had almost done him a terrible injustice.

Summer school, it turns out, was probably one of the best things that could have happened for Jameson. Instead of just eking by in algebra, he got the chance to get a really good grade in the class. He began geometry with a solid foundation and a tutor who can answer any questions. The academic reward bolstered his confidence. To this vested observer, it appeared he enjoyed being in charge of his own destiny.

Jameson gained a lot of knowledge about algebra and life this past summer. I also learned a valuable lesson. I can't fix all of his problems. More importantly, I learned, I'm not supposed to.

It sounds trite, but I wish that last year someone had said to me, "You need to let your son go and grow." I worried about him needlessly. And this hovering Mom could have hindered her child for perhaps another year, maybe even a lifetime. Who knows? I want Jameson's future successes to be his. Now I need to let go enough that the mistakes can be his as well. I've done a good job raising him, and it's time to allow him to begin accumulating his own memories, triumphs, even losses. It's also time for me to stop hanging on to Jameson's every breathing moment. He and I are both experiencing a new found freedom. I'm excited for him. I'm also excited about my own metamorphosis. Perhaps I'll take an art class, write more poetry, or splurge on a personal trainer.

Something very profound happened in school this past summer. Jameson and I both learned that mothers watch their children grow up. They don't do it for them. Its' a delicate equation no math class can ever prepare you for. My very own mother stepped in and guided me when I needed her most. I'm reaping the rewards of the joy, the pain, the pleasure and the sacrifice that motherhood is all about. Looking back, I see that my mother was so right. I am eternally grateful I didn't miss out on this sometimes trying but otherwise magical experience.

My mother's wisdom about saying and doing the right things at the right time is what's driving me, now just as it did fifteen years ago. This life lesson was much bigger than a summer of algebra. All my fears of a year ago about not being able to find my child on the public school campus in the massive sea of faces—well, they're gone.

When I pick Jameson up these days, he's easy to spot. He's the confident, self-assured, good-looking young man standing tall in the crowd. He shines in the sea of faces.

JOYCE MITCHELL

Joyce Mitchell prides herself on being a mother and wife as well as professional career woman. She received her M.A. degree in 1984 and has been a broadcast journalism lecturer at California State University, Sacramento, since 1989. In addition, Joyce has enjoyed a successful career as a news/documentary television producer. She's won three Emmy awards for her twenty-five plus years of work and is committed to using television to help make this world a better place. Delivering her one and only child at age forty, Joyce feels she almost missed out on the miracle of motherhood. She maintains her son is the best thing she's ever produced.

MAKING
a list

The face in the mirror looked miserable. Multiple chins obscured a once-elegant neck. Eyes were mere slits, obscured by baggy flaps of skin but, blessedly, no wrinkles. Fat filled those out. At age fifty-five, after years of living as an extra-large woman in a skinny world, after years of claiming I was content in my body, happy with who I was, I finally faced the truth. Fat was killing me.

The diagnosis of Type II diabetes and high blood pressure earlier that year, two years of sleeping sitting up because I could not breathe lying down, and dozens of failed diets had at last convinced me to do something about my weight. The birth of my son's baby cinched it. I wanted to dance at my granddaughter's wedding, and at nearly 300 pounds, I could not even walk up a flight of stairs, much less whirl around a dance floor. I researched weight loss surgery for a year, but had not yet decided to go through with it. This physical exam was just to see if I qualified. The doctor had just called.

Today the face in the mirror looked stunned. I had just gotten the news: breast cancer. I had not expected this. There was no cancer in my family. No diabetes, either. Or sleep apnea. I could not die yet. Too many of my dreams were unfulfilled. Too many experiences put on hold already. Too many failures and now, it seemed, no time to rectify them.

I had experienced humiliation, embarrassment, shame and disgust because of my weight. I was a chubby child and a chunky preteen. I lost weight in high school then gained it after I married. By the time I decided to leave my husband, I was officially obese. I lost fifty pounds after the divorce, then started dating.

That was my ultimate downfall. I kept choosing the wrong man time after time. I stopped trusting myself to make good choices and, consciously or subconsciously, decided that if I was unattractive, no man would ask me out, so I would not have to make those choices.

It worked. It also lost me jobs and made me a semi-recluse. Going out was too humiliating. I had to ask for tables instead of booths at restaurants; I had to take aisle seats at movies so I would not have to sit with my arms crossed; I took up two folding chairs at events and was not comfortable in chairs with arms. I'd even had a man ask to move rather than sit next to me on a plane.

People made rude comments. Sales clerks either ignored me or dismissed me. Black became my favorite color, loose and baggy my favorite fashion—not that it hid much. I stopped swimming, one of my favorite activities, because appearing in public in a bathing suit brought whispers and stares. My family and friends were constantly recommending diets and exercise plans. I tried some. None worked for very long.

The truth was that I did not care. I had convinced myself that I was happy. I claimed I wanted people to like me for who I was, not what I looked like. Some did. Others never gave me a chance. I found that I had to work extra hard for credibility; that I had to shine extra brightly to be taken seriously. I avoided cameras, mirrors, and large reflective windows—it was just too shocking to see that fat broad with the double chins and bulging, sagging breasts. I learned to make fun of myself before others could.

Nine months later, after a lumpectomy and weeks of radiation, after suffering blistering burns under my right breast and mind-numbing exhaustion, and after being brave in front of everyone but crying myself to sleep every night, I was ready to change my life. The oncologist had pronounced me cured—or at least temporarily repaired. It seemed absurd that I would subject myself to another dangerous major surgery, this time to reconfigure my internal organs, cut them apart, and staple them back together, just to lose weight. But the statistics were real—obesity had caused every one of my life-threatening conditions. Diets did not work for me. I was determined to be healthy again.

I made a list of all the things I wanted to do in a year. Some of them were fun: skydiving, hiking, taking a long cruise. Some were practical: buckling a seatbelt, fitting in a theater chair or airplane seat, shopping for clothes in any store, wearing a bathing suit in public. Some of them were pure fantasy: being whistled at, going on a date, enjoying having my picture taken, being noticed. It seemed impossible that any of these things could happen; for years, life as a fat person was the only life I had known.

I was used to being ignored, passed over, disregarded, insulted. It was amazing how being the largest person in the room made me invisible. Maybe that's why I had put on the layers in the first place: to avoid being noticed, avoid making hard decisions. My divorce had been a blow to my ego, and dating again a pure disaster. I had married young, quit college, and, after ten years in an unhappy marriage, had to raise a young child on my own, but I could only qualify for entry-level jobs. So it became easier to take myself out of the dating game rather than make bad choices; easier to blame my lack of promotions or job opportunities on other's prejudices about fat people than my own inadequacy; easier to be overlooked than be expected to shine; easier to put my dreams on hold. Was this surgery another easy way out?

Truth was, I was just as afraid of success as I was of failure. Failure was comfortable—after all, I had been a failure for years. As a chunky child, I failed at sports, always the last to be chosen, always the bench warmer. As a pudgy preteen, I failed at being popular; as an obese adult I failed at diet after diet. My plans for college failed, as did my marriage.

For years, food had been the only control I had in my life, the only way I knew to cope. What would I do with all those emotions and feelings and fears that I had smothered or hidden with food and fat? What if the surgery succeeded? That was just as scary as failing yet again.

Now, ten months after the surgery, the face in the mirror was more wrinkled, but lean. The triple chins were gone, the eyes wider, the cheekbones defined. I slowly turned around, watching the slender body reflected there. Who was she? I did not know. But I was determined to find out. The surgery and recovery had been uneventful, but my life had changed forever. My elderly father had passed away the previous month. His failing health, and mine, had defined my existence for eight years. I was his cook, housekeeper, nurse, and live-in caregiver and now my job was done. My son and granddaughter had moved to another state. And I had a whole new body.

Who was this person in the mirror? All my self-concepts were gone. I was no longer a caregiver. That role was done. I had not worked outside the home in almost a decade. My office skills were outdated. My grandchild was a thousand miles away. I was no longer a daily part of her life. My comfort in being invisible was gone. People noticed me now, talked to me, asked my opinion, opened doors for me, waited on me in stores. Last week a roofer had whistled as I passed by. I was the only person on the sidewalk. I had glanced at the store window and did not recognize the pretty, confidant woman reflected there. Was this really me? Even my friends did not recognize me anymore. I thought of my dreams—of traveling, building my dream house, dancing at my granddaughter's wedding. Could I do this? Sell my house, move to Oregon, take that long-postponed cruise?

For the first time in years, I wanted to live life again. This was my chance. I picked up the phone and dialed the realtor. It was time for me to step out on my own and find out what was waiting for me. My "to-do" list was long and it was high time I got started.

R. KATHRYN BERNHARDT

Kathy Bernhardt is a mother to one and grandmother to one and one half. She married and divorced young, raised her son on her own, survived breast cancer, major surgeries, cared for her ailing parents for eight years and is eagerly anticipating whatever life throws her next. Always positive and upbeat, she charges through life with a well-honed sense of humor and a faith that all experience only makes one stronger. Kathy is a wildlife rehabilitator and shares her home with an ever-changing menagerie of sick, injured, or orphaned birds.

SPICE
it up

Why did I say yes to that crazy tournament? Honestly, why was I driving 300 miles, staying two nights in a hotel, just to play bridge? Plus, I'd be traveling with three prissy old ladies, decades older than me. But they flattered me. They raved about what a fine player I'd become. How I would help my partner garner the points she needed for her master's level, or whatever you call it. And I'm a sucker for flattery. Besides, my partner was footing the bill, and I felt the need to escape for a few days.

Boy did they fool me, those old gals.

You see, after the last evening, after the last rubber had been played for the tournament, we settled ourselves back in our hotel. They flounced around the suite in their fancy peignoir sets; I slouched around in my sweats. With the wine flowing freely—they'd each brought a bottle—everyone became quite silly. The ladies and I let our hair down. Way, way down. Well, Isabelle took hers off; she wears a wig.

Anyway, the subject came up concerning the outrageous vocabulary that today's young people so casually use. We had just overheard some spicy conversation in the elevator between two young women, and that was the catalyst that sent three dignified ladies, and one almost dignified lady, into decadency.

Mabel said, prissily I might add, as only an aging Southern belle can be prissy, that she could never utter that "F" word; said she'd choke on it. Well, I couldn't let that go. I told her she was being an old woman and that I admired young people's freedom from convention. As you can imagine, a very lively conversation followed. I popped the cork on the second bottle and poured it around.

I would like to be able to say that I was the one who offered the opening gambit, but despite all my bluster I'm really awfully proper. No, it was Irene, as she sprawled back in a chair contemplating her swollen ankles. Right out of the blue she let fly with a comment about her "effing" arthritis (though she said the real McCoy), and how she shouldn't wear high heels at her "effing" age. She was so serious when she said it that the rest of us were shocked silent in seven different languages. Then she looked up from the study of her feet. She wore a naughty little smirk.

That did it! We laughed. We whooped. We howled until tears washed mascara rivers down our rosy rouged cheeks. When Isabelle caught sight of herself in a mirror she joined the fray by saying that she looked an awful "effing" sight. Now this was especially hilarious, mostly because it was true. Isabelle, wigless, and with her dissolving eye makeup following the path of least resistance through the gorges and canyons of her face, was truly an awful sight.

My contribution came after I'd cleansed my face and run a brush through my disheveled hair. My girl at the salon had made a mess of my last haircut, so I screwed up my courage and proclaimed how she had "effed up" my "effing" hair. I'd snagged a twofer, as they say.

This started a new round of howls and giggles, which caused Mabel to get the hiccups, which in turn caused the rest of us to laugh even harder. Mabel, always the dignified debutante, was having a hard time maintaining her decorum while trying to suppress those idiotic sounding hiccups. Of course, I had to tease. Laughing, I said, "Go on, Mabel, say it. 'Effing' hiccups. Don't be such a prude. Come on, Mabel, live a little. Say it!"

She glared at me, a look meant to incapacitate. Then she punctuated that look with another hiccup. She slapped both hands over her mouth in perfect simian imitation of speak no evil.

Need I even elaborate on how comical she looked? We showed her no mercy. We hung on each other and laughed until we fell to the beds. I had to stuff the pillow over Isabelle's face, she was making so much noise. Mabel drew herself up to her full height, sent a baleful look around the room, hiccupped, and said, "Y'all just go on and *'eff' off.*"

Oh my God! She did it! Well, what followed became quite ridiculous, we four gals wallowing in uncontrolled ribaldry.

We tried to outdo each other. Mabel, Lord knows where she ever heard some of the language she used, by far outshined the rest of us. Mercifully, our inner clocks, not to mention the third bottle of wine, finally put us down for the night.

In the morning we avoided each other's eyes. I picked up the empty bottles and dropped the evidence into the trash. Isabelle ordered coffee from room service, and while we waited for it to arrive we studiously watched *Good Morning America* each with our lips locked tight. After a cup or two of coffee, we sneaked a few quick peeks at each other. Talk about some sheepish gals. But I could see the twinkle in the eye and the twitch of the mouth, which could have started the whole thing up again. We promised, however, never to tell another living soul about our behavior.

So, you're wondering, why am I spilling the beans? Well, I want to tell you my side of it, just in case you ever run into a sweet little old lady who has a story to tell about a rude woman in her forties.

This is what happened.

Mabel and I went over to tournament headquarters to check on the results from last night's bridge. Mabel was standing just behind my right shoulder; of this I was sure, positive. We had played dreadfully. Then, thinking I could lighten the mood, I said over my shoulder, "Just look at those fucking scores, would you." I turned to catch Mabel's reaction. Instead, much to my surprise, I found I was looking into the shocked, blinking blue eyes of a sprightly little silver haired lady whose mouth made a perfect O.

There I stood in my Ferragamos and my power suit looking every bit like what I was, a forty-eight year old career woman. But that night's escapade had taught me a lesson. We may need help climbing stairs, as my companions do, or may worry about falling down and breaking a hip. Or, if we haven't quite arrived at that stage, we have other things to worry about, like our falling jowls and growing waistlines. But there is no reason to listen to what society dictates and stay locked in the cages of our age. None of us ever quite loses the spirit of feeling young. I could tell from the smug expressions my companions wore that morning that they felt younger than when we set out on our trip. I know I felt younger, and more liberated, and more hopeful for what the future holds as I reach the age of my three new friends.

And, that little silver-haired lady? She's out there. Oh yes. At every tournament I ever attend, that tiny dowager may be in the room giving her partner the elbow and saying, "That's the one, there. That's *her*!"

Oh yes, she's out there. And if I see her? I'll wink.

CLAIRE MCLEAN

Claire McLean lives and writes from her perfect paradise in rural Idaho, where her muse, unfortunately, is often AWOL and splashing barefoot in the creek behind her house. Claire's fiction has appeared in numerous literary journals. Currently, you may read one of her stories in the *Bylines Calendar*, 2006 edition. She has completed her first novel, *The Only Way*, and is at work on her second.

LOOSENING
the knot

Moving aboard a small sailboat meant leaving behind the accumulation of stuff that had clung to me over the years. I scrutinized every vase and jar, knick-knack and what-not for future importance in my life and asked myself, "Does this item have meaning for me?" The bits and pieces that failed the test, I labeled $5 or fifty cents; a thirty-seven-foot sailboat is small for full-time living.

Parting with my belongings was a bit like walking on ice. One by one, household treasures marched down the driveway. With each dollar that went into my pocket, the future seemed increasingly precarious and uncertain.

I am not a woman who likes the sharp, jagged edges of change. I prefer that things run smoothly, down the middle of the road. That is where I feel safest. But as I approached my fiftieth birthday, with my daughters off to college, it was time to make a change.

In a similar place in life, some women choose to sell their home and buy a condo. They want to paint, take up the harmonica, or learn to roll perfect pastry. But I wanted to write, learn a foreign language, and visit the Galapagos Islands, New Zealand, and Ireland.

With that in mind, the first project was to sell my land-based belongings. Once I began that process, I realized that my relationship to things was changing. When I was young, I didn't care what bauble was on the coffee table and sighed impatiently outside the gift shops while my parents fussed over buying a lavender hurricane lamp or a brass lantern. They debated exactly where the treasure would reside, on which table it would be enthroned, prior to every purchase.

But when I was slightly less young and on my own, my "stuff" became a great deal more important to me. Maybe this was because I had earned the money to buy each newly important thing, or because it defined the adult I was becoming. I happily acquired furniture to fill larger homes and fancier stuff to cover the tabletops. The addition of children added an entirely new world of shopping opportunities: from cribs and strollers to prom dresses and letter jackets. There was always more to buy.

But in middle age something was happening. I didn't want to be a slave to dusting. I wanted to live differently, with fewer possessions. And that's what the big yard sale was for. I was in the process of de-nesting, losing the excess baggage. Regardless of the nostalgia for a collection of old 78s or a once-prized golf trophy, I was ready to move on.

The experience reminded me a bit of my divorce so many years ago, when wedding gifts, treasures, and belongings simply walked out the door and into the moving van with my first husband. He took what he wanted, a small truck-load, and left me with the echoing space, dents in the carpet, and two babies. Then, as now, it was things, or the lack of them, that defined a major change in my life.

The lesson came back to me as I arranged my treasures on tables in the garage. Change can be seen as an opportunity or a disaster; it can be seized joyfully or not. That is a choice. Two decades ago, when I suddenly had less furniture, my little girls gained the space to ride their tricycles in the living room. Since that experience with disconnecting from my belongings had turned out to be positive, I faced this midlife challenge with equal optimism.

My piano headed down the driveway on a trolley. I turned to sell something less meaningful so that I wouldn't think about the magnitude of the increasing emptiness surrounding me. The series of sales consumed five Saturdays and a lifetime of treasures. I was left with a pocketful of cash, some empty card tables, and a nearly empty house, which was also sold. The spaces echoed. But I was free to embrace my new life full of possibility, with no stuff in my way. I was definitely headed in a new direction.

Living aboard *Nanook*, I enrolled in classes called "Medicine at Sea," and "The Offshore Cook." My second husband and I took part in a weekend seminar demonstrating rescue-at-sea techniques. I took scuba-diving classes and got a ham radio license.

With an anti-climatic toot of the horn we left our home marina, waving to friends on the dock until they disappeared from view. We stowed the dock lines and left the United States, headed south and west toward Mexico. We were going to sail around the world.

Our suburban lifestyle had involved a cycle of work-and-spend that kept us on the capitalist treadmill. Stepping off the corporate pedals created a shift. Now we intended to live by wind power and our wits. Part of the shift was realizing that what had been important in our land-based life was irrelevant on board a small sailboat in the middle of the ocean.

Daily mail, telephones, cars, and televisions didn't exist. The things that we had thought were necessities had become obsolete. I communicated via ham radio with other boats and occasionally to a shore-based message relay volunteer. I learned to use electricity conservatively because *Nanook*'s supply came from batteries that stayed charged through the solar panels or running the engine. Mail was forwarded in bundles every couple of months. We didn't even have pressure water or refrigeration. And once we made the adjustment, we didn't miss them.

Landlubbers are incredulous that a person can live, and live quite nicely, without such modern conveniences. I kept eggs in their boxes in the hammock with the breads. Simply turning the egg carton over every few days rotates the air pocket in each egg and reduces spoiling. In our years on board *Nanook,* I only tossed a few bad eggs into the sea. Cabbage keeps well unrefrigerated if the leaves are torn instead of cut with a knife. Jam and mayonnaise don't need refrigeration as long as the spoon is clean with each insertion. And cheddar cheese preserves itself nicely in a container full of olive oil. Since I had no way to store leftovers, when we caught a large fish we invited everyone within radio range to dine in our cockpit.

The boat's head was so tiny that a cotton-braided placemat served as wall-to-wall carpeting. We flushed the toilet with a long handle reminiscent of a casino slot machine. To keep the plumbing hoses clear, I poured vinegar into the bowl to dissolve the salt build-up that turns the insides of the hoses to cement.

My values changed. At sea we were entertained by dancing dolphins in the daytime and an umbrella of stars overhead at night. I took great delight in simple things that I had taken for granted or ignored on land. When the wind blew from the right direction, it meant a comfortable point of sail and a break from the diesel engine.

While underway we showered on the bow, pouring a bucket of salt water over our heads. I knew in my land life that a bar of gold Dial soap would repel deer from my garden, but living on a boat I needed new knowledge. I learned that Joy liquid dish soap is a cruisers delight because it lathers in cold salt water. At anchor, I indulged in the luxury of gently lowering myself into the ocean for a bath, followed by a freshwater solar shower. I wrote in my journal: *"Rolling waves lift me up for a view of the beach and drop me back into my private trough. Soap bubbles refract into little rainbows around me. I'm a child again and I splash with pleasure."*

We slept quite comfortably for our seven live-aboard years in the boat's 'V' berth, with our toes snuggled together but our shoulders far apart. We attached custom-made canvas storage panels to both sides of the sleeping berths. I designed them with large pockets so they held Kleenex boxes, journals and pens, magazines and other treasures.

I changed in small increments over the years of our travels. And like a jeweler reshaping a precious piece of metal by hundreds of small taps with a forging hammer, the events of our time-out slowly shifted the way I viewed myself and the way I related to those around me.

The grace I found in my travels took my life in new directions. I woke up to the concept that there are lots of beautiful ways to spend a day. The ways that I knew were simply that. The comfortable patterns I had established for managing a day were simply familiar habits and not necessarily my only choice.

The more villages I explored, the more I wanted to see. I embraced the joy of making new friends who were equally unhurried: sharing books, unbridled time, and tall tales. I learned to cook using the unfamiliar ingredients I could buy in foreign markets. The more the corners of my mind were pried loose by new possibilities, the more I yearned to explore. I learned that "home" is a concept—not a street address.

Through the experience of immersing myself in new geographies, I changed. I'm gaining a glimmer of understanding foreign cultures and what it means to think very differently from American cultural priorities. I no longer presume that the American way of being is more right than another. We work long hours and take short vacations. We buy big cars and new furniture. We buy so much that we need to rent storage space for all the extra stuff. We buy frozen food and unripe vegetables because efficiency is our mantra. We believe that those who are on time are better people than those who are late. These are American ways of being.

Traveling slowly taught me that there are other lovely ways to live.

As a result of my wanderings I'm becoming a writer, taking piano lessons, and learning snatches of foreign languages. I'm less afraid to fail. I am more forgiving of myself and of others.

I embarked on my intentionally homeless path to see if I had the skills—and the nerve—to make a radical change. I wanted to breathe the essence of each culture I visited, to participate in it. I didn't want my life to whip past me at sixty miles per hour and in the end realize that I'd missed the view. Years on the boat gave me that slow pace and allowed me to come back to land with a bigger perspective.

In the process of living with fewer belongings and suburban conveniences, I bumped into the realization that something in me had loosened, the way a knot loosens. Over the years, without noticing it, I'd subscribed to the notion that a crowded life was the same thing as a satisfying life. Now

I'm discovering the difference. I am becoming the person I want to spend the rest of my life being.

CHRISTIE GORSLINE

Christie Gorsline shoved self-doubt overboard and scribbled in journals for seven years while sailing the Pacific Ocean. She floated ashore and embarked on a 14,000-mile motorcycle adventure through Europe, eventually setting up camp in the mountains of Idaho. A freelance writer, Christie teaches skiing, takes piano lessons, and organizes a popular annual writer's conference on the shores of Payette Lake, *www.payettelakewriters.org.*

THE NEW
normal

It was one of those ordinary yet good mornings. We'd just returned from a weekend visit with an old friend. As a newspaper reporter, I had a nice daily story lined up so there would be no floundering at the week's start. Fresh from my bath, I was pulling open my lingerie drawer when suddenly it felt as if someone had yanked my legs and arms out in front of me. I heard a thud as my back hit the wood floor. The world went black.

My husband tells me that he came running when he heard me fall and unsuccessfully tried to rouse me before calling 911. All those female fantasies about being rescued by handsome firefighters failed to come true. Stark naked, stiff as a board, I didn't cooperate when my husband tried to get me into my pink robe. I heard and saw nothing until I felt a fireman lift my head with both hands and call out my name. His face was hazy and encircled by black, then gone.

They thought maybe I'd had a stroke. I don't remember being carried on a stretcher down the stairs by four ambulance attendants. I vaguely remember the oxygen mask being pulled over my face in the ambulance. I rallied enough in the first of two emergency rooms to look around but was unable to talk. My husband was told that I had a brain tumor that had caused brain swelling and the seizure. At my first meeting with my neurosurgeon, I asked, "Just how young are you, anyway?"

My skull was peeled open like a can of sardines and the lemon-sized tumor was removed. Looking back, I realized I had minor seizures that I'd dismissed as the flu. The nightmares I thought were due to hormonal changes were seizures, too. A week later, I was home again. A fourth of my hair on the right side was shaved. More than 120 stitches had sealed my skull shut. I was one of my surgeon's easy cases. Other patients were referred to me for encouraging advice. My benign tumor was gone.

The shock gave way to a slow physical recovery. First, a walk with only one dog at a time around one block. Our arthritic and aging Labrador and I walked at the same pace. My long afternoon naps got shorter. Finally, I donned a smart hat and attended my husband's shareholders' meeting. Slow and steady, picking up the pace, decreasing the medications, working more hours, looking and feeling more normal. It seemed manageable, accomplishable. Just like a difficult news series on an overwhelming topic like domestic violence or hunger. If I kept my focus, biting off one issue at a time, putting the pieces of recovery together just like a difficult story, I could envision the final product.

Until one day eight months later. My hair had grown and a stylish cut covered my four-inch scar where the stitches left a jagged part in my hair. Reporter's notebook on my lap, I sat in a hearing room at the state capitol. I noticed the television crew scooting in at the last minute, envying them their late arrival. I looked back at my notebook, then the air rapidly drained from my lungs. A wave of hiccup-like motions heaved from my chest, as if my lungs were trying to vomit. I had no more breath left but was still heaving nonetheless. My head started jerking down and to the right as if trying to duck under a fence.

Just like a horror movie when you think the monster is gone only to be startled into screams. It wasn't over yet.

The first "episode," as I call them now, landed me in the state capitol's nurse's office. A doctor from the hearing on our country's rapidly aging population was summoned to look me over. No one seemed too worried. I heard the nurse mention panic attack on the telephone to my doctor's office. My husband, whom I'd called from my cell phone, drove frantically downtown, not knowing what had happened.

After a few more episodes, the physical symptoms became isolated from the ensuing panic. At a Saks Fifth Avenue outlet, I clutched an armful of summer fashions and stumbled to a bench in the shoe section until it passed, then headed to the dressing room. Months followed filled with meditation classes, reading material on posttraumatic stress symptoms, lessons about midlife challenges, more time at home to rest, and therapy to figure out how to deal with all of it. What was due to hormones or disrupted sleep, and what was caused by age or overcommitment of time to work, social, and family events?

I spent time waiting for the next appointment with the neurologist, the next medical test. Waiting for the next breath to be stolen, the next words to get stuck in my throat, the next time I had to drop something from my hand to summon my husband for his comforting hug until the episode passed. The strange whiff of cigar smoke that came from nowhere. The worst were the episodes during sleep when I sat up in bed, screaming, arms flailing at the air to fight the unseen intruder who had stolen my breath.

It was almost anticlimactic when the diagnosis of epilepsy was delivered. The partial epileptic seizures were due to the injury to the brain caused by the tumor. I went back on heavy medications, which were more easily handled at home, waiting for my hair to grow back, than in a newsroom where life moved at a rapid pace. One day, a ladies lunch turned into some kind of nightmare scene where everyone was whizzing around like Vespas on the streets of Rome while I plodded along trying to keep up.

Mornings started at my desk in the newsroom, chugging caffeine while waiting once again for the fog to descend after the morning dose of antiseizure medicine. Not to worry, the doctor says, there are many more to try if the side effects don't fade. Waiting at the DMV office to hand over my suspended driver's license until a medical reassessment. A disagreeable woman behind bulletproof glass vague about the process or time involved in getting it back. Waiting for someone to take me to work or take me back home; waiting at the bus stop with the others disenfranchised from the road.

It was my first glimpse of disability in a mostly charmed life. A list of unrun errands in my purse, walking the treadmill to get away from unopened e-mails, unreturned phone calls, ignored letters, unable to think of what comes next but still aware enough to know that it matters.

My usual midday hope that my thoughts will be clearer tomorrow. The sequence to the day, the story, my life will come into focus. Occasionally there is a moment of clarity but not enough, not nearly enough. Hoping the next adjustment of medications will work. Whining to my therapist, "I just want to be normal again."

"This is normal now," she says. Maybe for now, I think, with renewed determination, but not forever.

NANCY WEAVER TEICHERT

Nancy Weaver Teichert is a news reporter who covers aging for the *Sacramento Bee*. During her thirty-year career at several newspapers, she has won many national awards for her coverage of poverty, hunger, child abuse, and social issues. She worked for the *Clarion-Ledger* in Jackson, Mississippi in 1983 when it was awarded the Pulitzer Prize for Public Service for the newspaper's coverage of public education issues. A native of Bloomington, Indiana, she is a graduate of Indiana University, married to Fred Teichert, a stepmother to his three daughters, and grandmother to four grandsons.

ROCK MY
world

"*Do you want* one cookie or two?" I could not believe those words had come out of my mouth and that they had been directed at my husband, who at the moment was staring at me as if I had lost my remaining marbles. The worst had finally happened. My world had become so small that I saw everyone in it as a child, and I was the nurturing, protective, doting mother.

I enjoyed being a stay-at-home mom. I read *Woman's Day* and *Family Circle* and had done so ever since each issue cost only a nickel. I religiously clipped recipes and coupons. The kitchen drawer was crammed with recipes for meals I would never create, cooking not being one of my strong points. Coupons were neatly filed in their proper envelopes, to languish until they expired. Once a year or so I cleaned them out and vowed to be more responsible about saving ten cents here and twenty-five cents there. I had fallen into a routine of predictability. Occasionally, however, I indulged a secret inner self and snagged a copy of *Cosmopolitan,* which gave me a glimpse into a world as foreign as Kuala Lumpur. Cosmo tantalized and teased, its quasi-pornographic monthly tribute to cleavage hinting at a world of possibilities for those of us daring enough to face the world with unfettered breasts. I never could figure out why cleavage was the major attribute on the cover of a magazine written for women, and always felt a bit embarrassed buying a copy at the grocery store. Still, there was an allure. Those women were different.

I was forty-two years old in the autumn of 1989, and while the great cookie gaffe was not the stuff of which movies were made, it was my defining moment. Pathetic, in fact, as epiphanies go, but it forced me to take a good, hard look at what my life had become. Self-analysis was painful, and I came up short. In a word, I was stagnant.

My children were nearly grown and spending little time at home. My husband was deeply involved in his professional career as a veterinarian, and I was doling out cookies like an intellectually bankrupt Mother Hubbard. What had happened to me? I had become invisible. I was John's wife. I was Evan, Heather, Park, and Keri's mother. I could only define myself in relation to other people. Somehow, somewhere along the path of wifedom and motherhood, I had misplaced myself. It was no fault of my family. I had done this to myself. But I realized with startling clarity that I deserved more and they deserved better.

What to do about the situation had me perplexed. Should I go back to work? I wasn't qualified to do anything. Well, maybe filing. That sure sounded exciting. Maybe I should go back to school. I could become an attorney. I had always rather liked Perry Mason, but the idea of defending the slime of the earth didn't sit well. I had originally planned to be a professor of history in a small, yet prestigious college, where I would write scholarly articles, perhaps even a text that would become the definitive work in its field. That plan had belonged to a different life. So I procrastinated. If I were going to make myself over, it would be only after deep reflection. After all, it had taken me fourteen years to arrive at this point. I had plenty of time to plan the next fourteen years.

Mother Nature, however, had set a plan in motion. If a gentle nudge had proved insufficient to jolt me into action, she had something of greater magnitude in store.

The kids were not home yet from school. John was at work, and I had finished the dishes and tidied up the living room. I was sitting with a cup of coffee at the dining room table. Notepad at the ready, pen in hand, I was returning to my new hobby, designing my future career. This was also becoming a part of the daily routine, and as long as the future remained in the theoretical arena, I could delude myself with a false sense of forward motion. I preferred this new occupation to coupon clipping.

At precisely 5:04 P.M., the earth threw me off my rear end and out of my chair, depositing me on the hardwood floor. It was October 17, in the San Francisco Bay Area, and the earth, having absorbed all the stress it could handle, made the logical next move and did a fair impression of an Amazon warrior with PMS. Ma Nature had thrown a 7.1 temper tantrum and, looking at the room from the perspective of an earthworm, I gained a sincere appreciation for her capacity to vent. Timbers had cracked, glass had shattered, and I was Paulette on the road to Damascus. Time was passing me by, and I finally understood what I needed to do. The slight bump on my forehead was the outward sign of the inner transformation. I had been shaken into action with a hearty thump on the noggin and a bruise on the posterior.

There are always dishes to wash, laundry to do, and housework to complete. But only one life and who would care if, at the end of mine, I'd let some of it go. So I did. And after all was cleaned up and post-earthquake life had resumed its onward course, I took my first steps into a different world.

I began by reading newspapers and books. A simple step, really, but it had been years since I had read for pleasure, and books had always been part of me. Why had I stopped? When had I stopped? I decided to enroll at the state college nearby and pursue a teaching credential. It would take two years, with some night courses and a few during the day as well. I became an alternative student, part of a growing movement of women reentering the world of work. Pleasantly surprised to find other women my own age attending classes, I formed friendships with kindred spirits and felt myself once more keeping rhythm with the heartbeat of life.

I taught for twelve years after earning my credential, but I never totally forgot what I had originally set out to do. It didn't take another earthquake to move me along on that path. Once was more than enough for that wake-up call. Instead I made myself a promise.

"In five years, Lord willing, you will be fifty-five years old. Will you be fifty-five with a Ph.D. or fifty-five without? If you don't do it now, you will never do it. What'll it be?"

One of the advantages of having a sincere conversation with yourself is that there is no one to argue with you, so of course I won the argument. Once again I pulled out the application materials, updated my curriculum vitae, and sent off my papers to the University of Idaho.

Five-year plans are nifty creations. Far enough out there to be doable, close enough to force some forward movement. So for the next five years, while I continued to teach high school, there were night courses and papers to write and lectures to attend.

And every year I came closer to my goal.

I traveled. As my expertise grew, opportunities presented themselves as well. I traveled to the People's Republic of China on a teaching standards delegation. The same year, as a Fulbright Memorial Fund Scholar, I visited Japan. And when I received my degree in December of 2002, my husband was in the audience cheering, my biggest fan.

It took longer to accomplish my goals than I had originally anticipated back in 1970 in Columbus, Ohio, where I had first attended graduate school. Thirty-two years longer, to be precise, but dreams deferred are not dreams denied, as there is a time and a place for everything under the heavens. You just need to know when that time is.

Today I continue to teach, although this year I teach as a visiting professor at the University of Idaho. There is some filing associated with the job, and filing is tedious. Sometimes I feel like an attorney, advising students about the legalities involved in the teaching profession, and I lament the loss of our innocence and the advent of the litigious society we have become. Filing and law, two early options I considered and discarded, still play a part in my daily career chores.

But what a ride. I have come so far since my cookie days. Today, I think, I would grab the whole bag and chew away. There are plenty of cookies for everyone.

KAREN BREES

Karen lives on a ranch with her husband, John, in a mountain valley in western Idaho. She raises South African Boer goats, quilts, gardens, and has just completed her first novel, which she hopes will become a *New York Times* and Amazon.com bestseller.

MORTALITY

sucks

August 28, 2002. I remember it well. It was the day my butt fell.

The morning began as usual, as I showered, had my coffee, and dried my hair. Then I climbed into my snazzy pair of Levis. *Damn,* I thought, *these really shrunk in the dryer.* So I pulled and stretched and did a few squats, but still the jeans felt tight. I berated myself for drying them on the wrong cycle. I untucked my shirt to see if that made a difference, but something wasn't right. I turned around and checked out my behind in the mirror. *It's the pockets, they're not in the right place.*

Then it hit me. It wasn't the pants. It was my ass.

I gasped. *Can't be. How could this happen?* I pushed up my rogue cheeks in an effort to get them to their proper position, but this only confirmed the worst. Gravity had become my reality. My butt fell, and I knew it.

What I didn't know was that a single gravitational atrocity would start me on a three-year spiral into feminine madness. Bad enough I was nearing middle age, did it have to be made worse by my being forced to shop for new jeans?

A few weeks later I turned forty. On paper it didn't bother me, but by the time my own personal nuclear winter set in, I realized that forty didn't mean I was living a full life—it meant I was half dead.

My butt fell and I was half dead.

With age forty, harsh reality set in. What the hell went wrong? I was supposed to be a fabulously wealthy writer living in an Italian villa surrounded by gorgeous men who incessantly purred around my ankles while expounding the virtue of sexually experienced women. Instead, I was doomed to wear elastic pants and slip-on shoes with enough traction to let me push through all the other broads clogging up the Hostess aisle at Wal-Mart.

There is no justice in life. And that was never more evident to me then during my fourth decade on what I'd sarcastically termed Planet Hell.

I never expected life to be easy, and that's a good thing, because for all intents and purposes it never has been. Like many women, I've always paid for my room in the karmic hotel by fighting the good fight, despite the constant pressure of external forces bearing down on my East German swimmer shoulders. At the very least, I could get up in the morning, look at myself in the mirror, and know full well that my conscience was clear. Now I looked in the mirror, got mad as hell, and lamented my bad luck while at the same time berating the universe for my sagging cheeks.

And so I spiraled. Not only did my butt fall, but my job prospects fell as well. After a hard fought twenty-two year career of winding my way through the battleground of female workdom, I became an obsolete soldier. All the work I'd been doing for my entire adult life was now being done in other countries. I don't know if I was more stunned or disappointed. Had this occurred in my thirties, youthful energy and logic would have forced me to remain chipper, but not so in my forties. Not only was I half-dead, but for all intents and purposes, I was ruined. And I still couldn't fit into my jeans.

Drowning my sorrows in caffeine, I thought long and hard and came to the conclusion that after forty, women just know. They know perhaps for the first time in their hurried lives that they're mortal. That's what I took issue with at the time, and still do. It's a tough revelation to swallow.

So I tossed the jeans, refused to buy new ones, and pondered my destiny on an hourly basis. The more I pondered, the angrier I became, and after a year of floating in the mire of devastation, I was bitter. Women are masters at holding grudges, and I had a grudge with the world. I call those my pessimistic years, but in truth it went far deeper than that. Personal ruin will do that to an individual no matter how emotionally or physically tough she is. I found that out the hard way, as even my deepest reserves of strength drifted like so much sand in Death Valley.

As with all things in my life, I attempted solace in humor. Okay, I'm dust on all accounts, where am I blowing? Where is the second half of my mortal life leading me? And when I get there, will all that is truly sacred to me still be within reach? Most importantly, will I find a pair of friggin' jeans that fit?

In some ways, I liken the mortal transition to shopping for shoes. In my twenties, I'd find the perfect silver sequin stilettos and think, "Wow. Those look comfortable. I can wear them forever." In my thirties, I'd find a great pair of little black heels and think, "They're not *too* high, I can wear them for my next dinner party." By the time I hit forty, I was debating over $10 Keds, wondering whether or not they were washable.

Podiatric fate, as well as denim, has a midlife turning point as well.

Those women who have kids perhaps feel their mortality sooner. I don't have children in the traditional sense— mine all have four legs and either bark or purr. Nonetheless, it matters not, for I still sense my mortality through my devoted pets. It's a horror to outlive your children. It's also a horror to outlive your best pair of jeans.

The concept of mortality and imminent death is arguably different for an unmarried childless woman. I became wrought with thoughts of my death and the mark I would leave behind. Would anyone even know I existed? Would anything I'd ever written be read long after I croaked? Would I have made a lasting impact on the next generation? At my funeral, would my friends tell everyone the tale of the day my butt fell?

With my mortality in question, I continued searching for answers. During my year-long hissy fit of coming to terms with forty hard-fought years under my belt, I thought "Okay, it can only get better. Life is still hard and every endeavor a challenge, but I can do this."

That was until my feminine physique became Dante's Inferno.

Men . . . oh . . . pause.

The irony is inescapable.

Here I am fighting for survival in daily life only to have yet another wrinkle in time tear through my demonic land of woe. How is a woman who is fighting with the concept of her mortality and her Levis supposed to put out a five-alarm fire with the equivalent of a medicinal squirt gun?

Menopause is evil. It's like your very own twenty-four-hour-a-day personal tropical vacation, only without the piña coladas, romantic dinners, and handsome cabana boy. Any ounce of personal sanity I was desperately trying to regain went straight down the loo. Tears did nothing but stuff my nose. Even chocolate offered zero comfort. At that point, I knew it was bad.

The most pressing issue was, ironically, another evil deed of vanity. Where the hell did my terminally flat stomach go? It's as if overnight I had become a dead humpback who washed ashore after a forty-year swim and was now bloated and baking on a sandy beach, much to the delight of camera-crazed looky-loos. At this point, the only thing that became perfectly clear to me was my propensity for elastic pants. Elastic pants. What sort of karmic chicanery is that?

So with dreams of my Italian villa fading fast, I had to wonder why it is that women are made to suffer in such a manner. Is it not enough that we've lived through periods, pantyhose, garter belts, hot pants, childbirth, and men? The affliction of menopause does nothing for the mortality factor. At best, it gives you keen insight into the concept of going postal.

"You have pre-menopausal symptoms, Miss Karg."

Lovely. Bless your little Amish heart for letting me know that for the next three to five years I'm going to roast in my own skin like the slowest trout in the pond. Thanks for the revelation that not only is half my life over, but the next half decade is going to turn me into an emotional teeter-totter constantly tormented by bloating, insomnia, migraines, and the overwhelming urge to alternately hug or kill anything that dares approach.

And by the way, I'm half dead and I can't fit into my jeans. Don't call me "Miss."

Desperate for advice, I crack and confess my ordeal to my younger sister. Of course being a younger sister, she dutifully explains that if these were pioneer times I would be a shame to my parents. A fortysomething single, childless woman living in today's modern world would, by pioneer standards, be a barren spinster living in the parental attic. Oh, and she gleefully reported that Wal-Mart was having a sale on elastic pants.

So much for sibling support.

So what is a female supposed to do? My inner Aphrodite is screaming to get out, but my outer bag lady is organizing a cellulite summer camp on my rear end. I'm at the crux. The parting of the "Dead" Sea.

Not only is this a dilemma of biblical proportions, it's downright vexing as well.

What do you do when you're too clumsy for yoga, the thought of wearing Britney Spears jeans makes you retch, and you don't want any surgical procedure done to your body that contains the words "suction" or "tox?."

At that point, I was not only broke but hormonally hosed. There was never a show called *Fortysomething*, and now I understand why. Apparently no one wants to watch a bunch of estrogen-imbalanced chicks pitifully lament the loss of their size-ten Levis while at the same time preparing afternoon tea for the Grim Reaper.

So with physical and denim mortality on the line and a consistently expanding belly, I attempted to justify my place in the universe. So what if all my work has gone to a sweatshop? There's nothing I can do about it. Hormones obviously eliminate a career in prostitution. Am I just supposed to roll over and die?

If you simply choose to roll over and die, then aren't you giving in to your mortality? I never was a woman who appreciated losing, but if I was to lose then I'd damn well better have given my best and been gracious in my defeat. But there's nothing gracious in regard to mortality or in buying a new pair of jeans. It sucks and I knew it, and as such decided to carry on.

In principal, I gave energetic thought to the bionic logic of the late seventies. I can make me better than I was before. Better. Stronger. Faster! But who was I kidding? I know myself better than that. I'm more apt to watch a creature feature marathon than run one.

Baby steps.

From cradle to grave, it's all about baby steps. Nothing in life is ever free, and nothing comes without strength and belief in oneself. So I believed. A year later, I'm nowhere near my Italian villa, but I do have a comfortable pair of elasticized jeans.

Mortality is a strange and constant bedfellow. I don't like living with it, but I'm not stupid enough to think I can avoid it. Instead, I've given myself permission to continue dreaming that I'm immortal and that I still fit into my Levis. Life is too damn short, and dreams are a terrible thing to waste. In reality, I may no longer be the Athena I once was, but that doesn't mean I still can't love, live, and fight with the best of 'em.

Forty isn't half dead—it's half alive. Perhaps I needed my butt to fall and my body to purge all those pesky uterine demons in order to wipe the slate clean. To this day I can't say that I'll look fondly on that particular time of my life, but it's my pain and I own it. What truly extends beyond financial ruin, bodily function, and denim dedication is that fact that I'm a woman, and women can survive anything.

I may be a flash in the pan now, but I take heart in knowing that somewhere, a comfortable pair of Levis is out there just waiting for me.

BARB KARG

Barb Karg is a career journalist, graphic designer, and screenwriter. She has authored and coauthored seven books. Her most recent endeavor is *Letters to My Teacher* (Adams Media, 2006). She resides in the Pacific Northwest with her better half, Rick, and their entourage of four-legged children.

THE FEAR

factor

When he spotted the climbing wall in the park downtown, my eight-year-old pleaded with me. "Can I climb it, Mom, please?" he begged. "You could do it too. We could go at the same time."

But I wasn't interested in heaving my forty-five-year-old body up a bumpy wall, clutching brightly colored fake rocks bolted into its surface. This was a kid's sport.

"No way," I told him. "I'd probably kill myself."

The man in charge fastened Morgan's harness, clipped him to the safety rope anchored at the top, and urged him on. I plopped into a folding chair, shaded my eyes from the low sun, and watched my son climb.

While Morgan made his way up one side, a man about my age, the father of one of the climbers, plodded up the other. Although not as fast as the kids, he climbed deliberately, studying the foot and handholds, choosing the best route. Eventually he made it to the top and rang the bell. When he looked down I could see his huge grin all the way from my seat. He had made it look simple; maybe this was something I could do after all. For years I've been watching my kids try new things. Now it could be my turn. The line was short; I wouldn't have time to talk myself out of it. So before I could change my mind, I jumped up and planted myself next to one of the walls.

As the manager helped me arrange the harness, I watched Morgan rappel as fast as he could. He simply kicked away from the wall, and because the cord allowed only a moderate descent, he glided down like a butterfly landing on a flower.

The father, on the other hand, pushed out, spun around, and crashed sideways against the wall like a pendulum gone haywire. Spinning his way down, he finally reached the ground, legs buckling underneath him. He landed with a soft thump on his rear, laughing at himself.

Maybe I was making a mistake. Viewed from the bottom, the wall looked higher than it had from the folding chair. Maybe this really was a kids' sport. But it was too late; I was already buckled in, committed. I placed my left foot on a large pink foothold, grabbed two blue handholds and hoisted my 150 pounds up the wall. My right foot found its hold, and I stood three feet above the ground.

I found the next foothold, but when my fingers slipped into the pockets of the handholds, I was startled; they were so small I could fit only three fingers in each. I pulled with my hands and arms, and again my body followed. Now I clung to the sandpaper wall six feet up. I felt strong. And it was kind of fun.

Ready for my third pull, I groped for another set of handholds. I found a small one again for my right hand, but nothing within reach for my left. I grabbed the edge of the wall, the thickness of a two-by-four, and heaved. When I looked down and saw Morgan twelve feet below me, a flash of dizziness made me press my forehead to the wall.

"Don't look down," someone below shouted.

I froze. I couldn't move up or down. I knew there was no way I could fall, but it was all I could think about. Falling.

My fingers ached deeply, and when I pulled one hand off the rock it trembled. I wiped sweat off each palm, one at a time onto my shorts, and felt for the next handhold. It was so small I could only fit two fingers in it.

"I think I'm done," I whispered. I felt around with my foot for a lower hold. But before I could descend, I heard a woman talking to Morgan below me.

"What's your mom's name?" she asked. When he told her, she shouted, "Go, Kathy! You're doing great!"

I was half way up. Good enough for a first time; I could quit now and suffer no shame. The muscles in my hands throbbed. I didn't see how I could go any farther. But it felt so good to hear her cheer me on; maybe I could make it just one more pull.

"Yeah, you're almost there. You're going to do it!"

I grabbed the edge of the wall and fit two fingers in a purple handhold, its center rubbed smooth by previous climbers. Now several people were calling to me, telling me where to put my feet, my fingers. "You can do it!" they cheered.

In that instant I felt part of something bigger. I felt a surge of power, and I pulled myself up one, then two more footholds until I was three quarters of the way. A little further and I, too, could ring the bell on top of the tower before rappelling gracefully back to the ground.

But standing there, clinging to the wall, I knew I was really finished this time. Now my arms were shaking, my fingers had stiffened into cup-like curves, and pain shot through my hands. It felt wonderful to get this far, so I wouldn't regret not making it the whole way. There would be another time.

"I'm coming down," I shouted.

"Okay, just kick out," the manager told me. I'd seen the kids do this. Kick and push out from the wall. Let your body weight drag you back to the ground. Float.

But I couldn't leave the wall, couldn't move up or down. Because I was afraid. Afraid of falling. I pressed against the wall, resting my cheek on its rough surface, waiting for my breathing to slow, for my hands to uncurl.

When did I become so fearful? When we were children, my brother and I competed to see who could hold their breath the farthest over the long bridges in Florida. Now, as I drove over bridges in the Bay Area, I clutched the wheel and fantasized how I'd have to break a window under water and swim to the surface of the frigid, murky water if my van flew over the short guardrail. If I survived the impact, of course. The immortality of youth has definitely left me, and now I'm more likely to ponder, even obsess over, my demise. How will I go? Hit by a car? A middle-of-the-night house fire? Incurable cancer?

Maybe it's because I'd leave behind two children that I fear dying now. I get tearful just imagining them attending my funeral. Or maybe it's that I'm reading obituaries for people my age, and I'm just not ready to go. I have way too much left to do, and I long for control over my fate. "That's too dangerous," I say to myself, even when I realize I'm missing something fun. "I could get hurt." When we were kids, a cast-covered broken bone was a mark of bravery, an enviable milestone. "Lucky break," we scrawled with colored felt-tip markers. "Good going," we cheered. But for adults, a cast—pristine and unmarked—is a badge of clumsiness, a symbol of foolish risk-taking.

Maybe it's just this whole aging thing. My body now is more often stiff than supple, more likely, I fear, to break than bend. My friends and I used to share adventure stories over dinner—scuba diving, bicycle trips, hiking on mountains. But now my mothers' group spends the entire appetizer course comparing aching joints and showing off new reading glasses. "When did we become our grandmothers?" I asked them recently.

I found the foothold below me on the wall and slipped down. "No," the man cautioned. "Kick out. Hold onto the rope and push with your legs."

But this meant letting go of the wall, and I couldn't do it. Instead I tried to inch down, but I lost my footing and started to spin, scraping my bare shoulder on the rough wall. I grabbed the side and righted myself, embarrassed at my graceless, slug-like descent. Finally, three feet off the ground, I grabbed the line, kicked out, and glided gently down. The short ride felt as if I was flying, and I wished I'd had the nerve to start from farther up. But I was too tired. There was no way I was climbing again today.

A week later, I watched Morgan and his friend, Marina, at their swim lesson. While Morgan treaded water, Marina stood at the edge of the pool. She shook her head when her teacher encouraged her to jump into the deep end. "I'm right here," her teacher said. "I promise I'll be here when you jump." From my spot on the bleachers, I could see Marina's face crumple. She was going to cry. She'd been performing cartwheels on the balance beam at gymnastics, but now she was afraid, and she did all the things we do when we don't want to go in the water. Deep breath. A half-step forward. Retreat. Start again.

I've struggled with when to intervene in kids' challenges. Do I let them do it on their own, or rush to "help"? What if my witnessing this humiliates her?

Then I remembered the woman's voice telling me I could climb that wall.

Across the width of the pool, I called Marina's name. I had to shout three times before she could break her trance and find me. I jabbed my thumb up and called. "You can do it!" She smiled shyly. "You go, girl!" I called. "You can do it." I saw her breathe in, straighten her back, and tighten her leg muscles. "Go, Marina!" I called. Would she do it? Would she jump or walk away, ashamed? She glanced at me one more time, edged closer to the water, and jumped. When she surfaced I let out a hoot. "Whooo! Girl! You did it!" Her smile was huge as she pulled herself out of the pool and jumped in again.

It was almost a year before I found myself in front of a climbing wall again. Ever since my virgin climb I'd wanted to try again, to see if I could get past the fear, or whether I'd have to accept that it was just too late for me to try something new, something risky, scary.

At the climbing gym across town, I stood at the bottom of the wall, staring up at the florescent green tape marking a beginner's path for me. I'd taken the belay course, learned to tie a figure-eight knot, and, just now, double-checked my carabineer. My rented climbing shoes pinched my toes, and already I was breathing fast. I was ready to climb.

"Climbing," I whispered to my partner, a young gym employee with a shaved head and a cobra tattoo on his forearm.

"Climb on," he said, and took up the last of the slack in the rope.

This time I climbed faster, buoyed by—and wanting to prove myself to—the professional at the end of the rope. He wouldn't let me fall. On my first climb I reached the top and patted the pulley, like I'd seen others do. It took a few more climbs to master the floating butterfly rappel, but it was my fifth climb that taught me what I really needed to learn.

Halfway up a purple 5.10 level course, I was feeling confident, proud that my upper body had been strengthened by a year of yoga, that my arms could pull my weight, letting my legs dangle, even if only for a few seconds. I was feeling tough and fearless and in the next instant I was hanging like a yo-yo that had run out of string. It happened so fast, I was never aware that my toes had slipped from their holds and I had plummeted two feet before coming to a springing stop, the cobra arm saving me.

I had fallen.

"Whooo, that was great!" I shouted down to my partner. Looking up at me, he smiled. "I did it," I called. A few others looked my way. "I fell!"

I spun slowly, sitting in my harness, rotating away from the wall. I was *not holding on* and it felt wonderful.

"I fell," I said again to myself. Then I turned to the scratchy wall, planted my toes, and hauled my forty-six-year-old body to the top.

KATHY BRICCETTI

Kathy Briccetti's work has appeared in newspapers, magazines, and anthologies. She is a student in the Stonecoast M.F.A. program in creative writing, and is at work on a memoir. Kathy lives with her family in Berkeley, California.

AUTUMN LEAVES
no fear

There I was, merrily bouncing along living my life with gusto, when the sixth decade slammed into my face. Totally unexpected, you understand. I mean, I knew it was coming, but I wasn't prepared at all. How does one do that, prepare to be sixty years old, when you feel like Peter Pan and still experience the joy and fairy-dust exuberance of youth?

The birthday came and went with the usual party, cake, and funny cards, and no particular angst on my part. It was later, a few days—maybe a week or so. The ever-popular leaf season had arrived, a time when I traditionally spend hours outside, raking and lugging leaves to create a mulch pile worthy of Mr. Bunyan.

After just three hours, realization hit: my yard-marathon days were over. Bones creaked, feet hurt, and the back of my neck oozed agony. Defeated, I crawled into the house and prepared to take a nice, long shower. I could give a long dissertation on what I saw in the mirror, but some of you already know that story. Wrinkles, lines, sags, and bulges: all were mine. That was no strange woman staring back. Just me in all my aging glory.

Yeah, yeah, I've heard all the yarns about old wood, wine, and books being the best. But did you ever notice that old wood becomes pockmarked with termites, aged wine bottoms out with thick sediment, and antique books crack easily and cast a sick, yellow glow? All quite unbecoming, I'd say.

This was a major depression here, something I surely had not counted on. I began strolling the shops, looking for skin creams and oils at the Lost Youth counters. I wondered if I was gray yet—I'd been coloring my hair for so many years, I had no clue. Perhaps if I left off with the dye and let myself be gray, fewer demands would be made on my poor old self. I wandered the shopping mall to buy nothing, just searching for I knew not what. I roamed through my house—dusty like me—and made mental lists on who would inherit what from my largess of knickknacks and clutter. I thought about cooking more. After all, that's what old women do: cook, while the old men putter. It's easier than doing nothing.

I imagined a stranger browsing over the obituary page. He sees my name, reads my age, and fleetingly thinks, "Ah, well, she was here long enough, anyway," and his eye rushes ahead to read the next name, searching for someone young so he can mourn for a moment.

Reading the newspaper myself, I noticed an announcement, "Free Flu Shots Tomorrow at Senior Center." Hubby and I agreed to avail ourselves of this bonus, so off we went. I had never been to the senior center before. It's a quite lovely building, with park-like grounds and very young workers. "I never thought it would come to this," I mutter.

We arrive early and begin to form a line against the wall. I am number twenty. Carefully, I watch as people assemble into the hall. Such an assortment of folks to examine. Some in walkers, some bent far over as though looking for a pin dropped on the floor. A few strut smartly, determined to show their vigor, while others shuffle along in their white athletic shoes. The dress code is eclectic: outmoded polyester slacks and sweat suits in bright, gay colors. Some outfits look very bedraggled and worn and one sprightly old fellow sports a Tommy Hilfiger shirt.

In comes Aunt Eunice, owner of the famous Eunice's Restaurant. She turned eighty last year—one year after some thugs beat her up and left her for dead on the city street. Our local television station did a whole series on her, as did the newspaper. Everyone rooted and prayed for her and she made it through the ordeal just fine, bringing home bags and bags of cards and gifts from strangers and friends. She still goes to work every day to bake biscuits and ham for her patrons.

Aunt Eunice wears a great grin on her face and orthopedic sandals on her twisted, bandaged feet. She is our poster-person for the State Arthritis Foundation and now I see why. Her big toe on each foot turns at complete right angles. How in the world can she smile with such painful feet? I admire that in a person.

Sitting on a bench across from me are two very old people. Together, they weigh less than I, but their smiles are much bigger. The woman is dark as night and her husband beside her has the look and color of my last cappuccino, very light, very sweet. Regally they sit, greeting all comers with handshakes and niceties. The lady does most of the speaking, "So very nice to see you again." Unconsciously, her arm reaches out from time to time to pat her husband's frail back.

Over by the door to the auditorium, where the shots will be administered, a man sits in a chair, laughing and loudly directing folks which way to go. He looks to be a bit older than me, and soon it's apparent that he is the son of the aged couple on the bench. He darts over each time someone comes to greet his parents to remind them just whom they are greeting.

The entire room is jolly with chuckles. No one grumbles about the long wait. I wish I was sitting on a chair so I could offer it to Aunt Eunice. It must be hard for some to stand so long.

Finally, we file into the big room and sit to await our number. I am seated just behind the little man and woman and their cheerful son. What a happy, happy fellow he is. Proudly, he tells us, "Pop is ninety-one and Mama just turned eighty-six." He helps his father off with his jacket and four sets of hands, mine included, reach out to help his mother.

I am glad to see the deference shown by the old to the older. There is something here I want, something I can look forward to. The young volunteer nurses seem to enjoy themselves. Everyone is laughing and smiling, and no one is in much of a hurry. This is leisure. This is life in the autumn years. My own won't have to be a marathon of wrinkle creams and oils, but instead a warm and caring time.

Thanks to our little visit to the senior center, depression falls away like autumn leaves, and I no longer fear my December.

LYNNE ZIELINSKI

Lynne lives in Huntsville, Alabama. She believes that life is a gift from God and what we do with it is our gift to God. With this in mind, she tries to write accordingly.

SEUSSED

Age—who cares? I certainly never did. Over the years I watched friends cry, moan, whine, and lament as they hit those landmark birthdays—twenty-five, thirty, forty. I'd even go out to commiserate with them. Sometimes I'd even pretend that it bothered me, but in reality, it was just another birthday. I didn't feel old.

Man, was I deluded.

I married at twenty-two and had my first baby at twenty-four. I became a stay-at-home mom, and, in truth, I enjoyed it. By thirty, I had three sons and two dogs. Female dogs. Surrounded by men, I refused to be the only bitch in the house.

By the time I was thirty-five, my youngest had started school, and I became acutely aware of the fact that I was brain dead. I knew all the words to every *Sesame Street* song, but I was clueless about anything that was in the top forty. I had every Dr. Seuss book memorized, but I hadn't read a novel or nonfiction book that didn't deal with child rearing in years. I could tell you what had happened in *Mister*

Rogers' Neighborhood today, but I knew nothing about current events or politics. The world had moved forward, but I was stuck in Play-Doh.

I don't regret staying home with my boys. I'm glad I did. Those years were important, for them and for me, and I would not change a moment. But I was never much of a soap-opera gal, and spending my days pondering which detergent would make my whites whiter and my colors brighter was mental death. What was wrong with me? How is that I could drool over alphabet blocks but I couldn't remember how to order a drink other than a bottle warmer? Was this what middle age had in store for me?

It all came down to a single dinner party. I hadn't been to a party in years, unless you count kids parties at Chuck E. Cheese, so I spent hours finding the right dress, fixing my hair and makeup, and cramming my feet into high heels. I was excited, but nervous. Could I hold up my end of the conversation? Would I be able to stay awake past nine o'clock? Could I refrain from trying to burp anyone?

We arrived at the party, and I grabbed a cocktail and headed for a spot at the edge of the room where I could observe the goings on. For a while I just smiled and nodded at others when they caught my eye. Listening to conversations around me, I was panicking. Then I caught wind of a gaggle of yuppie wives who were standing next to me. I overheard one of them say "Doctor" and "eggs and ham." Without a thought, I launched into it: "I do not like green eggs and ham. I do not like them, Sam I Am."

The gaggle fell silent. They turned and glared at me like I was ET's great grandmother. Only then did I realize that she was talking about some fad diet. I was mortified. I'd been Seussed.

It was right then that I decided to go back to school. I had started college years earlier and I had three years completed as an education major, but all those years of staying at home with my children made me realize I did not want to spend my days with other people's children. I'd sooner eat paste. So I went back to college, and changed my major to accounting. I'd always liked numbers—they're consistent, and they don't whine, throw up, talk back, or demand that you buy them things. It was an easy choice.

Despite the fact that I was pushing forty, I didn't feel old on campus. I fit right in. Sure, there were younger students, but there were plenty of older ones as well, and this time around, I wasn't interested in parties or guys. I was just happy to be around people who didn't need Underoos and wouldn't lock horns with me over a box of Sugar Pops.

As a forty year-old who graduated with honors, I was feeling pretty smug. Ha! I'm not living on *Sesame Street*! I'm not old! I can do anything!

And then I re-entered the work force.

What a shock! Suddenly my boss was my age, not older as it had always been. My supervisors were younger than me. Did I say younger? They were children. At every turn, I felt like I should remind them to wash their hands and do their homework, but instead, I had to go to them for assignments and questions. I had to listen to them criticize my work. After all these years, I was used to being the mom, telling my children what they should or shouldn't do. Now the shoe was on the other foot, and it was a bad stiletto nightmare.

How did this happen? How did the world pass me by?

Bad enough my supervisors were children, but my peers were babies. Literally, it seemed. The other cubicle dwellers in the staff room that we all called home were young enough that I could have been their mother. Every morning over coffee, conversation in the staff room would revolve around dates, concerts, and drinking. I'd stand there smiling, listening, all the while secretly stating:, *"What do you mean you slept with him on the first date? Your mother raised you better than that,"* and *"You drank how much? And you drove home? You idiot!"*

And then one morning it hit me. As I sipped my coffee and listened to a description of a weekend spent partying, I felt as old as Methuselah. The revelation fell on me like a cement truck. There was a time when I'd have been drinking, dating, and partying right beside them. Now I was mentally disapproving their youthful exuberance. This couldn't be right. I was only forty! That's not old. I was done using my uterus, but I wasn't in menopause. I didn't need a facelift. Oh sure, I was coloring my hair to disguise what I'd termed my *Horton Hears a Who Has Grays*. I did need glasses, but at least they weren't bifocals yet. I didn't even qualify for the senior citizen discount at Denny's.

Something was wrong here. I wasn't old. I wasn't going to let myself be old! So I set out to prove to myself that

I was still young—that I could still hold my own in this world of youth, that I wasn't ready for rocking chairs and bingo parlors. But what could I do?

My boys were all taking karate lessons at the time, so that evening, on a crazy whim, I joined the adult class. What was I thinking? Suddenly I was dragging my forty-something body that had been most taxed by pushing strollers and carrying diaper bags into a class where three times a week we would run, stretch, do push-ups and sit-ups, practice self-defense techniques, and spar. Spar? I ran home to watch a Bruce Lee movie just to know what that was.

I was forty. Could I spar?

By the next class, there I was, decked in padded helmet, padded gloves, and padded boots. I felt like the Michelin Man. A forty-something marshmallow who was going to fight eighteen-year-olds? Is this what happens when you get old?

There were only three females in the class. Our instructor believed that the only way to truly know how to defend yourself was to know that you would get hit, and if you had never been hit you would never be able to take a punch. So to make sure we all knew what it felt like to get hit, sparring meant only punches to the face would be pulled. Otherwise you hit, and you were hit. You kicked, and you got kicked. By the end of the first week, I was exhausted, bruised, and I felt like I'd been run over by a semi. I was also exhilarated.

I was a karate queen and I was holding court, but somehow that still wasn't enough. I was still feeling out of whack.

And then one morning it occurred to me. It was a thought so evil that I grinned all day—a grin that would rival the Grinch. By the end of the day I was a wench on a mission, and as I parked my car and glanced over at my destination, I was feeling the power. That tattoo parlor never looked so good!

A few hours later I was sporting a little rose on my hip. Not everyone could see it, obviously, but I knew it was there. My husband was in awe. A few months later I got a second one. This one was a butterfly on my thigh, and depending on what I was wearing, it showed. There I was—a respectable mom in her early forties, a certified public accountant, a past president of the PTA—with a pair of tattoos and a future black belt in karate. An old woman would never be doing those things, would she?

At work, I had always been included in the invitations to go out after work for a beer but I'd always declined, thinking the others were just being polite. But I was not old, damn it! They were inviting me, and I would go along. So one afternoon, when my coworkers said they were heading to the bar down the road for an after-work beer, I went along. Why not? I may have been having a midlife, crisis but I wasn't dead. After all, so far I'd avoided buying a convertible car, having an affair, becoming a drunken lush, and buying designer purses—all symptoms of a midlife crisis. So why not have a little fun?

By the time I hit my forty-fifth birthday I didn't feel old, and I didn't really care any more if my bosses and my coworkers were younger than I was. A great weight lifted off me on that birthday. I realized that I'd had a mini-midlife crisis, but that wasn't a bad thing. I hadn't hurt myself or anyone else. My middle-age mayhem had pushed me into improving myself. I got into a great exercise program and amazed myself with how much I could do. I made friends with younger coworkers and enjoyed having a few beers. I also saw things in them that helped me understand my own children as they grew into adulthood.

My pair of tattoos is a constant reminder of my inner beauty. In many ways the butterfly symbolizes my breaking out of the cocoon of my earlier years and emerging to fly out and do things I never thought I would, like graduating from college, passing my CPA exam, and earning my black belt in karate. All of those seeming obstacles had helped abolish my Dr. Seuss doldrums.

When I was in my teens, thirty was old. By the time I was in my twenties, old had moved to forty. In my thirties, old jumped to fifty. Now, at forty-seven, I'm thinking that there's no such thing as old.

ARJEAN SPAITE

Arjean Spaite is a certified public accountant and freelance writer. Her most recent endeavor appears in *Letters to My Teacher* (Adams Media Inc, 2006). She also won a state-wide essay contest on friendship among women. She resides in Ohio with her husband, three "mostly" grown sons, and two female dogs.

DON'T LET ME
be last

"*I want Jill* for my team. She's fast."
"I'll take Mary."
"That leaves Gwen and Carol. What a choice!"
Snickering followed.
"I guess I'll take Gwen; you're stuck with Carol."
I was mortified. Once again, I'd been chosen last. Would I always be last?

As a bookworm and unathletic kid, being chosen last for recess games or for physical education competitions left me feeling isolated and wishing the ground would open up and swallow me whole. It colored my opinion of my worthiness as an individual; I never felt I was good enough to fit into a world that valued being athletic over being intellectual.

Children can be cruel to those who do not fit their ideal, especially to those who are less outgoing and athletic who cannot dribble the ball and sink a shot like Michael Jordan, tackle an opponent like Lawrence Taylor, run like Michael Johnson, or hit a baseball like Sammy Sosa. I did not fit the mold. During my school years, I could usually be found with my nose in a library book. Getting caught by the teacher reading a novel instead of doing my class assignments just reinforced my bookworm label. My myopic eyes, hidden behind bottle-glass thick lenses, added to the role in which I had been cast.

Being chosen last became standard procedure. I dreaded physical education classes when group activities were involved. At least I was halfway decent in gymnastics and in sprinting short distances. When those were the day's activities in junior high, at least I didn't have to wait to be chosen last for a team.

Time passed. I graduated from high school and college, got married, began my teaching career, had two sons, and gained fifty unhealthy pounds over a twenty-year period.

Turning forty is a milestone for all women, especially to those who have packed on the pounds. Shopping for school clothes that summer shocked me into taking action when I realized that I was moving up to a larger size—a sixteen.

Determined not to let my weight control me, I began a walking regimen that I had used after the birth of my sons to lose the "baby fat." I hit the road at six every morning for a two-and-a-half-mile power walk and again in the evening for a total of five miles a day, seven days a week. In less than a year, I had shed fifty-five pounds, dropped to a size six, and regained a sense of pride in myself.

I had never been very competitive but I began entering races as a power walker. In my first 5K, which is 3.1

miles, my girlfriend and I entered for fun. Less than half-way through the race, my competitive spirit took over and I took off running—and won a third-place trophy in my age division for forty to forty-five year olds.

Three years later, I was still running and winning medals and trophies in some of my races. My greatest feat was competing in the Tulsa Run. By that time, I was not interested in winning trophies or medals but in achieving personal goals.

The late October day of the Tulsa Run dawned bright and warm. I had set my goal of completing the nine-mile race in ninety minutes. When the gun sounded and the crowd of over 10,000 surged forward, I could feel the blood pumping through my body and the burst of excitement as I started the race that changed my life forever.

For the first seven miles, a friend and I ran side by side to pace each other. As others passed us, we heard words of support, "You can do it."

"Way to go, girls."

"Keep on going, you are almost there."

My legs were aching from running on the concrete.

I wanted to give up, but I knew I couldn't.

Spectators on the sidelines clapped, cheered, waved, and shouted more words that boosted my determination to reach the finish line. Ah, the finish line. Would I ever reach it? Perspiration rolled down my forehead, speckled my face and fogged my glasses.

Suddenly a cramp gripped my side. Slowing down to ease the pain, I told my friend to go on without me. I didn't want to ruin her time, but I was disappointed. I wasn't going to make my personal goal.

I continued at a slower gait and those who continued to pass me called out, "Keep on going. You can make it."

As I struggled to regain some speed, an older man whom I knew by sight jogged up next to me. His grey hair pulled back in a ponytail and the lines on his face revealed the many journeys he had made in his life. Seventy-five years old and competing in his twenty-first Tulsa Run, Nocus McIntosh was a former track coach. I recognized him from the walking track back home, but I had never had a real conversation with him.

"Are you okay?" he asked.

"I'm fine except for this side stitch. It's easing up, but my time is ruined," I replied.

"Is this your first Tulsa Run?"

"Yes, and I set a goal of ninety minutes. I'm not going to make it I'm afraid," I replied.

"Doesn't matter," he said.

"Why?"

"Because what matters is that you had the guts to try in the first place. It doesn't matter if you don't reach your goal; you attempted to reach a goal—that is what counts in life. Setting a goal and working towards it," Nocus said with a grin.

As he finished this last statement, his longer stride moved him forward. Contemplating his words, I realized that my side no longer hurt. To heck with my time, I thought, I was going to finish this race.

Watching Nocus ahead of me, I picked up my speed again, determined to finish right behind the man who had competed in every Tulsa Run since its beginning. If he could do it at age seventy-five, I thought, I could finish the nine-mile run at my age.

Nearing the finish line, I felt a surge of adrenaline kick in. Focusing on Nocus, who had already crossed the line, I sprinted with all I had left in me. I wouldn't be the last to cross the line, but it didn't really matter. I had finished in ninety-seven minutes—only seven minutes over my goal.

Weeks later, as I added the newspaper clippings and photos of the Tulsa Run to my scrapbook, I recalled the small child who wanted to disappear when teams were selected, and I suddenly realized that I wasn't last anymore.

CAROL A. ROUND

Carol A. Round is a retired journalism/English teacher who resides in Claremore, Oklahoma, with her dog, Taco. In addition to writing a weekly faith-based column, she has been published in numerous national magazines and anthologies.

CHAIN SAW
mama

On a Saturday morning when she had hoped to sleep in, my daughter remembers lamenting, "*Wouldn't it be nice to wake up to the sounds of my mom in the kitchen making breakfast.*" Instead, she had been jolted out of bed by the dreadful racket of her mother's chain saw just outside her window. Other mothers were content to cook and sew. Her mother had to fix and build.

It wasn't always that way, though the signs were there early enough. I loved getting dirty and capturing frogs. I was the only girl on the sixth grade softball team. I got in trouble over the softball thing. The principal of the school (a woman) called me to the office one day ordering me to quit the team because in her words, "It isn't ladylike behavior."

The public school system brainwashed me again and again. In high school, shop classes were mandatory for the guys. Home economics classes were required of every future homemaker, and that meant girls. We learned to make nutritious meals and sew an apron or repair a zipper. I wanted to take shop classes but was told not to make a fuss.

My childhood was further mixed up with a mother who, though she never thought about a career for herself, introduced me to books like *The Feminine Mystique*. Author Betty Friedan was to rock American culture with the idea of "feminism," and I was part of the revolution—though I joined the race like the turtle not the rabbit, poking along in a ladylike fashion after marrying at nineteen and having my daughter at twenty-two. I was a homemaker. Oh Lord, this was my mother's life!

The shock of being an antique in a new age jolted me into action. I finished my education and launched into a successful career as a journalist. My career took off. This was no longer my mother's life, it was mine—sleek, new and fast.

I can't say I was surprised when my marriage ended—we had been so young at the start—but I can say I was startled by the new duties that came with being a single parent head of household. It's the middle of the night, for heaven's sake—who's going to make the toilet stop running? The sink's stopped up? The disposal's broken? *Duh . . . I dunno.* My leap from powerful woman to woman with power tools and do-it-yourself drive, took only a couple of bills; one for $86 to install a new toilet flapper and another for $246 to put in a new garbage disposal. I watched the guys do it and thought, *"This is not brain surgery. I can do this stuff."*

In the early eighties, the big burly men with dirty coveralls and ugly fingernails chuckled when I strolled into the local home improvement store displaying my ignorance along with my parts list for a project. Okay, at the time I didn't know what "eight inch on center" meant. Could have been some basketball term for all I knew. A Phillips screwdriver? Hey, I was buying one for me, Elizabeth. But I never let on I didn't know what I was doing. I just kept on trying one small project after another, mostly learning by my mistakes. I was so proud of installing a new showerhead and faucets in my bathroom. It didn't bother me at all that the hot water came out of the handle marked with a "C" and the cold out of the one marked "H." Little things like that added character to a house. Same with the new deadbolt. It worked fine after I installed it. You just had to know the key needed to go into the lock upside down. Maybe I planned it that way to foil a burglar with a set of keys.

I got better over the years. Not great, but my projects, like an older horse, could be described as serviceably sound. Never mind the handyman's motto "Measure twice, cut once." This handy*woman* was in a hurry. Measure once. Cut twice. That worked for me. I was comfortable with the conclusion I would never be a finish carpenter, but I did want to advance my skills. I tried new projects all the time.

I was doing fine on my own, and my daughter was learning just how capable women can be all by themselves. Just when you think you finally don't need a man in your life, one comes along to make you blink and blush and think again. You'll know I was really in love when you hear this man had three sons. Yes, that's right. *Three very young boys:* two, four, and six years old. And I got married a second time.

I guess I felt if I could unplug a drain, fix a leak on the roof, or repair a lawn tractor, what could be so hard about a bunch of kids? You can see that this same spirit saved me from being a helpless girly girl when the world was telling me that's all I could be. My new husband saw me as his trophy wife, but not for the reasons you'd think. He's a physician, on call every third night with no time to take care of the periphery . . . that periphery being home maintenance. He was proud to have me—Mrs. "I Can Do It"—on his arm. He needed that a whole lot more than he needed young and sexy.

The mom job was a bigger challenge. Just as my home-repair projects were less than journeyman quality, my parenting of three little boys was adequate but not superlative. We were all a little raw around the edges. I learned one mistake at a time, though truth be told, the boys added their own signature challenges on occasion. There was a lot of love along the way; like wall patch, I guess if you dab enough around broken places it's all good again.

We were crazy, though. We didn't just stop with my daughter and my husband's three sons—we added an "ours" to the chaos. So, in one year's time, I went from an independent life with an only child to managing a career, learning to deal with a doctor/husband whose patients came first, keeping track of five—count em! Christine, Matt, Phil, Ty, and baby Evan—plus the fix-it chores connected with a much bigger and older house.

It didn't kill us, so it must have made us stronger. Though Mary, my next-door neighbor, might argue with this assessment. Our kitchen windows faced each other over a narrow walkway that separated the houses. One summer day with windows wide open, I took on the task of replacing our very tired garbage disposal. There I was, under the sink with my tools, happy to be keeping a professional serviceman away from my broken stuff and my fragile bank account. I had studied the written instructions that came in the box with the new disposal. Though I almost didn't bother—nine times out of ten, the directions that come with any given appliance are so poorly written that only a certified mechanic can understand them . . . and even that's not a sure thing. Not understanding had never stopped me before, so I launched into my Saturday morning project.

By Saturday afternoon I was annoyed. Getting the old disposal out had not been easy. I had turned off the water to the sink, disconnected the hoses, removed the seal, and twisted the big disposal tank. It would not budge. I had to go to the local hardware store for advice and they sold me a tool made just for twisting these blasted things out. So who knew you needed a special tool? I counted it as just one more notch of knowledge on my tool belt. I finally got the old disposal out and my annoyance melted away. *"I can do this!"* Energy and attitude restored, I began the installation of the new disposal.

An hour later I was not annoyed, I was pissed, red in the face, blood pressure rising. The damn thing would not go into place. I tinkered, I fussed, I fumed then I started cussing. "Damn it to hell! You piece of garbage. You don't want to work! I'm gonna kick your butt and you're gonna line up right." I pounded on the disposal tank, even kicked it, then finally got it threaded and snugged up. I eased my head out from under the sink and came up for air, muttering now, wiping sweat from my forehead.

And there was Mary, staring into my kitchen window from hers with a look of horror on her face. I waved and smiled. Mary's hand flew to her mouth as she turned and fled. I suddenly realized Mary must have thought I was berating my poor husband—who of course worked very hard, just not at home, and certainly didn't deserve to have his ass kicked so he'd line up right.

Many days later I tried to tell Mary I had been installing a garbage disposal that had given me fits, but she looked unconvinced and regarded me suspiciously forever after. My husband still laughs at this memory now, many years later, and tells me how impressed he was that the garbage disposal worked perfectly.

Two years ago, my daughter called with a strained voice saying, "Mom, I'm so scared." Her two-year-old daughter had suddenly turned up with symptoms that had prompted a sprint to the hospital emergency room and a diagnosis of juvenile diabetes. Katherine's life would depend on careful blood sugar monitoring, insulin shots, and a strictly regimented diet. "Mom, I don't know if I'm strong enough for this. I feel like I'm falling apart."

"You can be scared. But are you up to this task? Of course you are," I said. "You have no choice. And besides you have untapped strength from that DNA I supplied. We're tough broads, don't you forget."

"You've been showing me all these years. I guess it's my turn to be strong."

And Christine never looked back. Katherine is healthy, active, and positive. Now, at age four, she confidently tells her preschool friends about her disease, explaining that she needs shots every day to replace the insulin her pancreas no longer makes. Big words for a little girl. And brave ones too, all because her mother has remained strong.

Being a handywoman has brought many rewards. My husband still adores his trophy wife as we move into semiretirement. My grown up children come to visit us at our ten-acre ranch, offering hugs and occasional help with my projects that are now centered upon three horses, a dog, cat, a house, and a garden. Katherine brags to her friends about coming to visit so she can ride my tractor. I'm proud to be a chain saw mama. There's only one thing better—a chain saw grandma!

ELIZABETH HOBBS

Elizabeth lives in the mountains of Northern California with her husband of twenty years and their pets. She treasures the peace and quiet of rural living, broken occasionally by the sound of a chain saw.

UP, UP, AND
away

"*Lucky early birds*, you get to see the balloon inflate," the driver says into the rearview mirror. I'm on vacation with my husband—just the two of us—for the first time in the four years since our kids were born. This weekend, there are no blocks to pick up, no carrots to chop, no garbage to take out.

The dark blue van with "Balloons Over The Valley" stenciled on the side crunches to a stop on the gravel. In the morning chill, white fingers of fog stretch across the vineyards. We jump out of the van, and head toward an enormous checkerboard of colors spread out in the muddy road. I squeeze his hand, and my husband Thompson tosses me a grin.

I set up this trip months ago: arranged for my parents to come babysit, booked a swanky hotel room, packed massage cream and incense. It's been far too long since I treated the father of my children like my lover. Too much routine, too much taken for granted, too much humdrum.

"Climb aboard," shouts our captain, and he deftly vaults into the large basket underneath the ten stories of color. A couple of guys help us up and over, and before I can even take out my camera, we leave the earth.

In a breath of a moment, with no fanfare at all, we are suddenly aloft, drifting silently, smoothly upward. I tilt my head over the side and look straight down at the rapidly shrinking people. My sunglasses slip down my nose and for a moment, I feel the vertigo of knowing I could fall, right this second, if I leaned out any further. I catch my glasses, tuck them into my jacket pocket, and back up, pressing into my husband. He's there, of course. And he curls his arms around me.

"Welcome to my office," our captain says, gesturing at the sweeping view of the Napa Valley. The sun peeks over the Vaca Mountains in the east, and I look up into our hot air balloon, a billowing riot of purple, green, yellow and red nylon that gently carries us southward.

"Wow," Thompson says, squeezing me around the waist.

As we float upward, our shadow gets smaller, an eighteenth-century shape darkening row after row of grapevines. I watch his face; he has freckles I've never seen before, a fresh haircut. The sun beams through the mist and creates a rainbow halo that encircles our shadow. He kisses my ear, "Thanks for this, babe."

We have not spent a day alone together in four years. It's been a dozen years since our first kiss, and we've made the transition from lovers to spouses to parents. But since our kids were born, our relationship has become more practical, more about the logistics. (*I can pick up Alex from preschool, but can you get Sofi to the pediatrician next Wednesday at 9:15? Would you pick up some soy milk on your way home?*) and less about the two of us. At night, after I've finally tucked the kids in and untwined their arms from around my neck, I usually tiptoe downstairs to unload the dishwasher, write a little, and pull the hot clothes from the dryer. By the time I get upstairs, he's on his side of the bed, breathing softly.

My husband is an easy man to be with. He'll pace across the squeaking floorboards, cooing our daughter to sleep. He'll get down on his belly to build expansive Lego cities with our son, snapping colored rectangles together. He doesn't sneer when my mom leaves eight-minute messages on our voice mail. He's low maintenance.

But his easygoing nature makes it easy for me to forget that the home fires do need to be tended. I have cruised along, grumbling about his underpants that perpetually miss the hamper, irritated when he forgets to put out the recycling. Even though he has told me he feels neglected, I have a hard time connecting with him in bed. Thoughts of garages that need to be organized and deadlines that loom flutter across my mind when he snuggles up to me in the dark, and I too often kiss him softly on the cheek and turn away. I cook dinner most evenings, and I rub my foot against his in the middle of the night, hoping that's enough.

But last night as we sat at a table lit with candles, a perfect linen napkin gracing my lap, a woman about my age cried at the table next to us. She told a woman I guessed was her mother about the ways her marriage had crumbled.

"We just don't like each other anymore," she said, her face creased with pain. She knuckled her forehead, "I don't even know when it happened."

This weekend I am remembering what it is like to be with my lover. For two whole days we are focused on each other. I'm not thinking about what time I have to take the chicken out of the freezer, or next Tuesday's field trip, or the editor I need to call. I gaze at the strong curve of my husband's freckled shoulder, the wrinkles in the corners of his eyes, his thinning hair. We are getting older, my husband and I, and he looks good to me, now that I'm taking the time to see him.

Thompson grips the edge of the basket when we swoop suddenly westward. My stomach flips over.

"How do you steer this thing?" Thompson asks.

"You don't," our pilot smiles.

Our pilot looks far ahead, the silver snake of the Napa River twining through miles of misty vineyards.

"Even on autopilot you have to watch all the time," he says. "It'll keep you at the right altitude, but you're at the mercy of the winds. If they shift, you get blown off course."

I think of the rough spots Thompson and I have been in over the years. We fought after our anniversary party a couple of years ago. I balanced our baby daughter on my hip, my milk-filled breasts gapping the new blouse I had bought to make me feel attractive, something special for our celebration. My husband's friend Yana was fawning over him, laughing loudly at his every comment, gesturing with her Cosmopolitan in the air. She announced that she'd certainly faint if she had to hold a newborn baby. He grinned and poured her another drink. I tossed back my shot of apple juice and went upstairs to change the baby. "How can you be so goddamned insensitive!" I screamed at him after everyone had gone home.

We drift along for nearly an hour, at times hovering only a hundred feet above the stone walls of a winery, then soaring to 2,000 feet so fast I feel my insides plummeting.

Our captain tells me, "There are wind currents blowing all over the place. At different altitudes, they're stronger or weaker, and blowing in different directions."

By going up, we catch the current he's looking for, and we head for our landing spot.

Back on the ground we brunch on champagne and strawberries, and we receive our Certificate of Ascension which states in curling calligraphy that "Suzanne and Thompson are adventurous souls, and have ventured skyward together."

"Up there, just riding the wind, it kind of made me think," I say, stroking my man's arm while we sit on the terrace of our hotel room at the end of the day.

"Marriage seems so effortless, but really, there's so much you have to pay attention to."

I rest my head against his shoulder, and breathe in the spring scents of lavender and olives that float on the evening breeze. "You can't just put a relationship on autopilot, or you end up in a place you don't want to be."

"Mmm hmmm," he says, closing his eyes.

We've made love, soaked in a tub, and now we're wrapped in thick warm robes, both of us drowsy and happy.

"And you've gotta shoot a hot blast into the canopy very now and then to keep it aloft." I nip at his earlobe.

He leads me to the bed, kisses my fingers and says, "You know what I really want to do?"

I cock an eyebrow at him.

"Let's watch *X-Men*," he grins, flipping onto his belly.

I laugh. And even though I could care less about a dumb movie, I grab the remote and turn it on.

A few minutes later, room service arrives, chocolate truffles wrapped in phyllo dough and a tiny oval of tarragon ice cream. We savor the rich dessert while mutant teens battle the government.

SUZANNE LAFETRA

Suzanne LaFetra is an award-winning writer whose work has appeared in the *Christian Science Monitor,* the *San Francisco Chronicle, Working Mother, Ladybug, Smokelong Quarterly, Rosebud,* and *Pearl.* Her essays have been included in eight anthologies, including the *Chicken Soup* and *Rocking Chair Reader* series. She lives with her family in northern California, where she is at work on a memoir.

JUMPING
at the chance

What was I, crazy? There I was, sitting atop a horse I barely knew, struggling to concentrate on what my riding instructor was telling me.

"Start with this little vertical here, Jenny," Martin began. "Turn right at the rail and come around to the brush jump, then go left and finish with the little picket fence."

"Okay," I replied. To myself I said, *Yeah, right!* I was fifty-two years old and a timid rider at best. What was I doing up on this unfamiliar gelding—a big one, at that—and about to ride him around a course of jumps?

I took a deep breath and pressed my legs into the horse's sides. *It's* because *you're fifty-two and a timid rider, remember?*

I guided the horse to the first jump. *If not now, when? At sixty?*

I hadn't always been timid. As a child, I'd ridden with the fearlessness of youth. If there was there a challenging mount in the lesson string, one that charged his jumps or threatened to buck, I wanted to ride him. A bad actor? Let me at him. At fourteen, I got my own horse, a three-year-old, green-broke Thoroughbred filly. Tigress and I grew up together, and she carried me through an awkward adolescence. I was shy and intense, the type that's known as a late bloomer. Until my braces came off and the contact lenses went in, I was pretty sure I'd never have a boyfriend, much less get married. But I had Tigress, and on her back I felt competent and powerful.

My next horse was not as good, however. A sly bully, Strider whittled away at my confidence, testing me by refusing my requests and threatening to rear. Over time, I began to question my abilities as a rider. Better horses followed, but by then, married and publishing a regional magazine, I had scant time to ride.

In 1983, my focus turned to starting a family. My husband and I had married in our early twenties, so we'd waited ten years before even trying to conceive. Then Hank and I spent eleven years in the effort, making our way from one infertility treatment to the next, even trying one round of in-vitro fertilization.

Nothing worked. In 1993, at age forty-one, I was told I was going into perimenopause. I struggled to come to grips with this prospect, then discovered, three months later—to my astonishment—that I was pregnant.

That put the kabosh on riding, for sure. Hank and I were elated, and after waiting twenty-one years for a child, I figured I could postpone riding for nine months. Darling Sophie arrived at seven months, however, so for the next few years I was completely absorbed in nurturing my little preemie. I sold my two horses—and the magazine—and settled happily into the life of a stay-at-home mom.

My dream, of course, was that someday Sophie would love horses, too, and we'd ride together. When she was three, we bought her a twenty-year-old miniature horse—a scant thirty-nine inches to the highest part of his back. Sophie loved Smokey; she could groom and lead him herself, and I'd walk beside while she rode him up and down the little hills surrounding our home in rural Northern California.

At six, she started proper riding lessons at a nearby stable, and by ten she was on her own third pony, a small horse-sized gelding she named Brego. In the meantime, I'd done little riding myself. Whenever I thought about getting back in the saddle, the anxiety Strider had planted in my heart more than twenty years earlier would flicker into fear.

It wasn't all his fault, though. Simply becoming a mother tends to make one more risk-averse—who'll care for the child if something happens to you? Plus, I was now over fifty, and let's face it. At that age, you just don't bounce back from falls the way you did at twenty or thirty. I'd also been freelancing for equestrian magazines, and all those articles on riding safety had left me fully aware of the many things that can go wrong.

Still, Hank and I believed enough in the virtues of horse involvement (terrific exercise, confidence building, character development) to let Sophie ride, and I kept telling myself I'd get back to it, too. Eventually.

The turning point, oddly, had as much to do with being fifty as it did with loving horses. Fifty is more daunting than forty. Fifty separates the women from the girls—literally.

My own forties had been relatively easy. My husband and I, always health-and-fitness conscious, had a small child to keep up with in that decade. She made us feel young. Yes, there were those lines on my face, plus subtle body changes I wasn't crazy about (so *that's* what they mean by saddlebags!), but overall I felt pretty good about myself.

Fifty, I came to learn, is a tougher go. Yes, you stop worrying so much about the wrinkles—because sagging jowls are a bigger concern. You trade running for walking, to ease the nagging pain in your joints. More significantly, you begin to lose loved ones and acquaintances at an alarming rate to death and disabling illness. These aren't older folks, either. These are people your own age. It gives you pause.

At fifty-two, as I pondered these realities, I began to take notice of the women who jumped horses with my daughter at Martin's Falcon Haven Farm. They ranged in age from mid-teens to sixty-something, and they were all strong and athletic—toned legs, sturdy cores, awesome arms and shoulders. Moreover, they were *brave*. They followed Martin's directives without hesitation, ever expanding the range and scope of their abilities. They also took setbacks, and the occasional tumble, in stride.

One pair in particular caught my eye. Brittney, sixteen, had been riding with Martin's barn for six years. Three years ago her mother, Jerry, had decided to join the fray. Now Jerry owns her own jumper and gives her daughter a run for her money; the pair sometime compete in the same classes at shows. And love it.

I yearned for Sophie and me to be like Brittney and Jerry. But for that to happen, I'd have to start jumping again . . . after a hiatus of thirty-five years, and in spite of my lingering fearfulness. From the beginning, Martin, sensing my interest, had been prompting me to ride Mogie, his retired show jumper.

"C'mon, Jenny," he'd said. "You'll enjoy the Mog-Mobile. He's forgotten more than most horses know." I was tempted, but though I occasionally rode Mogie on my own, on the flat, I couldn't quite screw up my nerve to try jumping him.

Then, in 2004, two things happened. In June, I lost one of my dear sisters to a stroke. Shelly was the oldest of the five of us and had been our leader. It was a terrible blow.

In October, Sophie and her pony went with Martin and the others to her first rated hunter-jumper show. There, from the sidelines, I had a chance to taste just how sweet "the horse thing" could be.

Whenever any of our group was riding in a class, the others trouped to the arena to cheer her on. Martin coached each rider directly before her round, then gave feedback and encouragement afterwards. When no one was riding, we gathered at our barn area, chatting and relaxing under a canopy. For horse lovers, it was heaven.

As I watched Sophie ride, then Brittney and Jerry and the rest, I could feel momentum building inside me.

You could do this! I told myself. *But you'd better get going. The clock is ticking.*

Before long, I was sharing Sophie's weekly jumping lessons. My first time out, on reliable old Mogie, was a revelation. After Sophie and I warmed our horses up, Martin set some ground poles for us to trot over, then one simple vertical. It was only about a foot high, but to me it was, figuratively, a brick wall. If I could get over it, I'd be into a whole new world.

Sophie popped Brego over the tiny fence, then it was my turn. Oddly, now that the moment had arrived, the butterflies were gone. The need to focus on the approach to the fence drove all other thoughts and fears from my mind.

I rode Mogie forward. He came within thirty feet of the jump, twenty feet, ten feet. "Now!" called Martin.

I closed the angle of my hip, bringing my upper body closer to the horse, and moved my hands forward, freeing his head and neck. Mogie sprang up and over, making a smooth arc with his long body. Before I could blink, he'd landed on the other side, then cantered off without a fuss.

I'd done it! "Yay, Mommy!" shouted Sophie. "Well done!" added Martin.

I couldn't stop smiling, and I knew I was hooked. As I continued with lessons on Mogie, I modified my search for a horse of my own. I'd been looking off and on over the preceding months for something on which to go trail riding with Sophie and Brego. Now I switched gears and began to look for a horse that could jump.

After many false leads, I found a handsome teenaged gelding with lots of jumping experience. I brought him home for a trial, and Martin pronounced him a suitable match. Killian's Red is kind and quiet, fun to ride, and exuberant when he jumps.

That exuberance is why, at my first lesson on him, I was having second thoughts.

"Go on," Martin encouraged. "Do it just as you do on Mogie."

I bring Killian around and square him up for the first of the three jumps. Three strides to go, then two, then I'm crouching low and giving him his head. Whoosh! His bound is quicker, more eager than Mogie's, and it startles me. But the horse—my horse!—comes back to my hand after the jump, and allows me to guide him to the next fence. We come in a little crooked, and Killian makes an awkward but successful leap. I collapse on his neck upon landing.

He stays steady as I reorganize, and before I know it the final fence is before us. Steady, straight, up and over—I've done it!

"Way to go, Mom!" cheers Sophie, waving her whip over her head with glee.

On our ride home, Sophie and I laugh and talk and compare notes. I think about this common language we now have, the language of horsemanship. Her teenage years are right around the corner, and I know this commonality between us will come in handy.

I also marvel at how "the horse thing" can clarify and energize routines that might otherwise be getting wearisome. For me, staying fit has always been about health, but also, to be honest, about striving to look good. Now, I find that looking good is a clear second to *being* good in the saddle.

Push-ups, crunches, squats—I need them now more than ever, to create muscles that can steady a galloping horse, secure my seat in the saddle, drive a distracted mount forward on a lazy day.

Flexibility work? It's essential, too—to sink my heels down, protect my lower back over jumps, and cushion my joints in the event of a fall.

Cardio? Absolutely. Jumping around a course takes a lot of wind, and it also builds wind. So riding has become a part of my workout routine.

As Sophie and I walk our mounts up the last hill before home in a companionable silence, I think about the other perks riding offers to a fiftysomething woman. Bad hair day? No matter—the helmet will flatten all, anyway. Just grab one of those hats you've been collecting but never seem to wear, and be on your way.

No time for makeup? The horses won't care, and people on the ground won't notice anyway. And on it goes.

Later, after we've put the horses away, Sophie and I head to town to run a few errands before Hank gets home. I'm still in my boots and riding pants, and I've slapped a wide-brimmed Panama over my sweaty head. It's perhaps not an ensemble I'd have worn in public in my twenties and thirties, but now I don't care.

Hey, it's what I do. I ride jumping horses.

JENNIFER FORSBERG MEYER

Jennifer Forsberg Meyer is an award-winning journalist and author. She writes a biweekly column, "The Rural Life," for her hometown newspaper, and a monthly column, "The Riding Family," for *Horse & Rider* magazine. The author of two books, she also produces the annual *Growing Up with Horses: Parents' Handbook & Resource Guide*. Jennifer lives in Northern California with her husband and their horse-loving daughter, Sophie Elene.